1900s
1910s

Decorative Art

RIGHT PAGE / RECHTE SEITE / PAGE DE DROITE:
Charles F. A. Voysey, Textile design, c. 1900

Editorial note:
The dates shown in the footers on the reprinted pages relate
only to the year of publication and not to the year of design
for the artifacts included.

Anmerkung der Herausgeber:
Die Jahreszahlen in den Kolumnentiteln geben das Erschei-
nungsjahr der Zeitschrift und nicht das Entstehungsjahr
der Objekte an.

Note éditoriale:
Les dates indiquées en bas des pages renvoient à celles de
publication et non à celles de création des objets concernés.

© 2000 Benedikt Taschen Verlag GmbH
Hohenzollernring 53, D–50672 Köln
**www.taschen.com**

© 2000 for the works by Peter Behrens, Georges
D'Espagnat, Albert Gessner, Ludwig Hohlwein, John
Jacobson, René Lalique, Robert Mallet-Stevens, Ludwig
Mies van der Rohe, Richard Riemerschmid, Gerrit Rietveld,
Wilhelm Schmidt, Heinrich Vogeler, Frank Lloyd Wright:
VG Bild-Kunst, Bonn

Design: UNA (London) designers
Production: Martina Ciborowius, Cologne
Editorial coordination: Susanne Husemann, Cologne
© for the introduction: Charlotte and Peter Fiell, London
German translation by Uta Hoffmann, Cologne
French translation by Philippe Safavi, Paris

Printed in Italy
ISBN 3–8228–6050–6

# 1900s
# 1910s

## Decorative Art

**A source book edited by Charlotte & Peter Fiell**

**TASCHEN**

# CONTENTS
# INHALT
# SOMMAIRE

# PREFACE

PAGE / SEITE 4:
Alberto Issel, Oak secretaire, 1901
PAGE / SEITE 5:
Casa Mayol, Cádiz, 1912
LEFT PAGE / LINKE SEITE / PAGE DE GAUCHE:
Josef Hoffmann, *Sitzmaschine No. 670* for J. & J. Kohn, c. 1908
BOTTOM LEFT / UNTEN LINKS / EN BAS À GAUCHE:
Hans Ofner, Silver basket, c. 1905
BOTTOM RIGHT / UNTEN RECHTS / EN BAS À DROITE:
Viennese carpet, c. 1910

## The "Decorative Art" Yearbooks

*The Studio Magazine* was founded in Britain in 1893 and featured both the fine and the decorative arts. It initially promoted the work of progressive designers such as Charles Rennie Mackintosh and Charles Voysey to a wide audience, and was especially influential in Continental Europe. Later, in 1906, *The Studio* began publishing the *Decorative Art* yearbook to "meet the needs of that ever-increasing section of the public who take interest in the application of art to the decoration and general equipment of their homes". This annual survey, which became increasingly international in its outlook, was dedicated to the latest currents in architecture, interiors, furniture, lighting, glassware, textiles, metalware and ceramics. From its outset, *Decorative Art* advanced the "New Art" that had been pioneered by William Morris and his followers, and attempted to exclude designs which showed any "excess in ornamentation and extreme eccentricities of form".

In the 1920s, *Decorative Art* began promoting Modernism and was in later years a prominent champion of "Good Design". Published from the 1950s onwards by Studio Vista, the yearbooks continued to provide a remarkable overview of each decade, featuring avant-garde and often experimental designs alongside more mainstream products. Increasing prominence was also lent to architecture and interior design, and in the mid-1960s the title of the series was changed to *Decorative Art in Modern Interiors* to reflect this shift in emphasis. Eventually, in 1980, Studio Vista ceased publication of these unique annuals, and over the succeeding years volumes from the series became highly prized by collectors and dealers as excellent period reference sources.

The fascinating history of design traced by *Decorative Art* can now be accessed once again in this new series, reprinted in a somewhat revised form from the original yearbooks. In line with the layout of *Decorative Art*, the various disciplines are grouped separately, whereby great care has been taken to select the best and most interesting pages while ensuring that the corresponding dates have been given due prominence for ease of reference. It is important to remember that the dates shown in the footers on the reprinted pages relate only to the year of publication and not to the year of design for the artifacts included. Finally, it is hoped that these volumes of highlights from *Decorative Art* will at long last bring the yearbooks to a wider audience, who will find in them well-known favourites as well as fascinating and previously unknown designs.

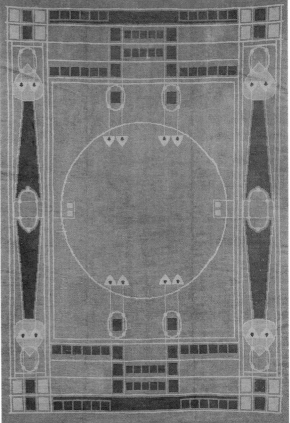

# VORWORT

## Die »Decorative Art«-Jahrbücher

Die Zeitschrift *The Studio Magazine* wurde 1893 in England gegründet und war sowohl der Kunst als auch dem Kunsthandwerk gewidmet. In den Anfängen stellte sie einer breiten Öffentlichkeit in England und in Übersee die Arbeiten progressiver Designer wie Charles Rennie Mackintosh und Charles Voysey vor. Ihr Einfluss war groß und nahm auch auf dem europäischen Festland zu. 1906 begann *The Studio* zusätzlich mit der Herausgabe des *Decorative Art Yearbook*, um »den Bedürfnissen einer ständig wachsenden Öffentlichkeit gerecht zu werden, die sich zunehmend dafür interessierte, Kunst in die Dekoration und Ausstattung ihrer Wohnungen einzubeziehen.« Diese jährlichen Überblicke unterrichteten über die neuesten internationalen Tendenzen in der Architektur und Innenraumgestaltung, bei Möbeln, Lampen, Glas und Keramik, Metall und Textilien. Von Anfang an förderte *Decorative Art* die von William Morris und seinen Anhängern entwickelte »Neue Kunst« und versuchte, Entwürfe auszuschließen, die »in Mustern und Formen zu überladen und exzentrisch waren.«

In den zwanziger Jahren hatte sich *Decorative Art* für modernistische Strömungen eingesetzt und wurde in der Folgezeit zu einer prominenten Befürworterin des »guten Designs«. Die seit 1950 vom englischen Verlag Studio Vista veröffentlichten Jahrbücher stellten für jedes Jahrzehnt ausgezeichnete Überblicke der vorherrschenden avantgardistischen und experimentellen Trends im Design einerseits und des bereits in der breiteren Öffentlichkeit etablierten Alltagsdesigns andererseits zusammen. Als Architektur und Interior Design Mitte der sechziger Jahre ständig an Bedeutung gewannen, wurde die Serie in *Decorative Art in Modern Interiors* umbenannt, um diesem Bedeutungswandel gerecht zu werden. Im Jahre 1981 stellte Studio Vista die Veröffentlichung dieser einzigartigen Jahrbücher ein. Sie wurden in den folgenden Jahren als wertvolle Sammelobjekte und hervorragende Nachschlagewerke, besonders auch für die Zuschreibung von Designern und Herstellern, hochgeschätzt.

Die faszinierende Geschichte des Designs, die *Decorative Art* dokumentierte, erscheint jetzt als leicht veränderter Nachdruck der originalen Jahrbücher. Dem ursprünglichen Layout von *Decorative Art* folgend, werden die einzelnen Disziplinen getrennt vorgestellt. Mit großer Sorgfalt wurden die besten und interessantesten Seiten ausgewählt. Um die zeitliche Einordung zu ermöglichen, ist das Veröffentlichungsjahr der gezeigten Objekte im Kolumnentitel angegeben. Dabei handelt es sich aber nicht um das Entstehungsjahr. Mit diesen Bänden soll einer breiten Leserschaft der Zugang zu den *Decorative Art*-Jahrbüchern und seinen international berühmt gewordenen, aber auch den weniger bekannten und dennoch faszinierenden Entwürfen ermöglicht werden.

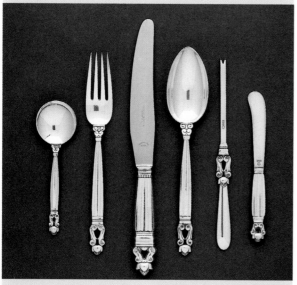

# PRÉFACE

BOTTOM LEFT / UNTEN LINKS / EN BAS À GAUCHE:
Louis Comfort Tiffany, *Pond Lily* lamp for Tiffany Studios, c. 1900
BOTTOM RIGHT / UNTEN RECHTS / EN BAS À DROITE:
Galileo Chini, Tile for Arte Della Ceramica, 1898–1902

## Les annuaires « Decorative Art »

Fondé en 1893 en Grande-Bretagne, *The Studio Magazine* traitait à la fois des beaux-arts et des arts décoratifs. Sa vocation première était de promouvoir le travail de créateurs qui innovaient, tels que Charles Rennie Mackintosh ou Charles Voysey, auprès d'un vaste public d'amateurs tant en Grande-Bretagne qu'à l'étranger, notamment en Europe où son influence était particulièrement forte. En 1906, *The Studio* lança *The Decorative Art Yearbook*, un annuaire destiné à répondre à « la demande de cette part toujours croissante du public qui s'intéresse à l'application de l'art à la décoration et à l'aménagement général de la maison ». Ce rapport annuel, qui prit une ampleur de plus en plus internationale, était consacré aux dernières tendances en matière d'architecture, de décoration d'intérieur, de mobilier, de luminaires, de verrerie, de textiles, d'orfèvrerie et de céramique. D'emblée, *Decorative Art* mit en avant « l'Art nouveau » dont William Morris et ses disciples avaient posé les jalons, et tenta d'exclure tout style marqué par « une ornementation surchargée et des formes d'une excentricité excessive ».

Dès les années 20, *Decorative Art* commença à promouvoir le modernisme, avant de se faire le chantre du « bon design ». Publiés à partir des années 50 par Studio Vista, les annuaires continuèrent à présenter un remarquable panorama de chaque décennie, faisant se côtoyer les créa-

tions avant-gardistes et souvent expérimentales et les produits plus « grand public ». Ses pages accordèrent également une part de plus en plus grande à l'architecture et à la décoration d'intérieur. Ce changement de politique éditoriale se refléta dans le nouveau titre adopté vers le milieu des années 60 : *Decorative Art in Modern Interiors*. En 1980, Studio Vista arrêta la parution de ces volumes uniques en leur genre qui, au fil des années qui suivirent, devinrent très recherchés par les collectionneurs et les marchands car ils constituaient d'excellents ouvrages de référence pour les objets d'époque, notamment en ce qui concerne l'attribution des œuvres à leurs vrais créateurs et fabricants.

Grâce à cette réédition sous une forme légèrement modifiée, la fascinante histoire du design retracée par *Decorative Art* est de nouveau disponible. Conformément à la maquette originale des annuaires, les différentes disciplines sont présentées séparément, classées par date afin de faciliter les recherches. On souligne au passage que les dates indiquées en bas des pages rééditées renvoient à celles de publication et non à celles de création des objets concernés. Enfin, on ne peut qu'espérer que ces volumes présentant les plus belles pages de *Decorative Art* feront connaître ces annuaires à un plus vaste public, qui y retrouvera des pièces de design devenues célèbres et en découvrira d'autres inconnues auparavant et tout aussi fascinantes.

# INTRODUCTION
## THE 1900s AND 1910s

LEFT PAGE / LINKE SEITE / PAGE DE GAUCHE:
Bruno Paul, Vitrine *Model No. 2616* for Vereinigte Werkstätten für Kunst im
Handwerk, 1903–1904
BOTTOM / UNTEN / EN BAS:
Charles F. A. Voysey, Brass ink-well, c. 1903

## The Morality of the New Art

The architecture and design of the early years of the 20th century were permeated with a new moral sensibility that had evolved from the teachings of earlier reformers such as William Morris and John Ruskin. Opposing the heavy ornamentation of the High Victorian style, designers aligned to the new movement pursued a more thoughtful approach to design that was for the most part based on the concept of utility with beauty. From their first appearance in 1906, the *Decorative Art* yearbooks echoed this sea-change by favouring designs that showed a "suitability for the purposes intended". They also provided a vital link between British designers and their contemporaries on the Continent and in America, who were able to follow each other's progress through the yearbooks' generous illustrations of new work.

*Decorative Art* offered not simply an annual overview of the latest currents in furnishing and building, but also sought to formulate some guiding principles for architecture and interior design. Thus it assessed the requirements of a house from a psychological as well as a physical point of view, with special attention being paid to sanitation, lighting and colour – all of which were believed to affect both health and happiness. Readers were also urged to seek a harmonious balance between colour and form that was neither too outlandish nor too dull. During this period, the fashion for antique furniture among the upper classes spawned a demand for reproduction furniture among the middle classes. The yearbook despaired of this vogue

for "slavish copyism", suggesting that it was injurious to progress and had a "narcotic effect upon industry".

Although the "New Art" style had initially been pioneered in Britain, by progressive architects and designers such as C. F. A. Voysey, by the turn of the century this reformist movement was evolving independently on the Continent, especially in Germany and Austria, where decorative extravagances were being replaced by simple functional forms. 1907 saw the founding in Munich of the Deutscher Werkbund, one of the first organisations expressly dedicated to reconciling artistic endeavour with industrial production. It would be another eight years before its British equivalent, the Design & Industries Association, was founded in 1915 – a telling reflection of the philosophical and economic ground that was being lost to the Continent. From its beginnings as a revolt against the ugly commercialism of the 19th century, the New Art movement now became an international phenomenon. As early as 1907, the term "Modern Movement" was being used in the *Decorative Art* yearbooks to describe this new and widespread style, which was anti-historicist in outlook and characterised by the use of simple, uncluttered lines. The New Art movement manifested itself in Britain most notably in the applied and decorative arts, and on the Continent in both private and public buildings, which were frequently conceived as a stylistically integrated *Gesamtkunstwerk* ("total work of art").

## Rural Ideals & Modern Realities

British architecture during the 1900s tended towards the picturesque and was generally sympathetic to its surrounding environment in terms of character, materials and aspect. While this was the heyday of the British country house, the country cottage was also much praised by architects and critics for its homely simplicity. Classicism was generally deemed an inappropriate style for northern climes and was described by *Decorative Art* as "artificial, cold and portentous", its symmetry also being blamed for a blandness of character. The use of stucco to imitate marble was particularly frowned upon as being untruthful. Instead, architects were encouraged to use local materials and to allow the exteriors of their buildings to be dictated by their interior plans. This in turn, it was hoped, would produce a

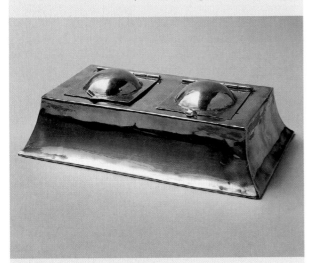

RIGHT PAGE / RECHTE SEITE / PAGE DE DROITE:
Ernest W. Gimson, Oak sideboard, c. 1906
BOTTOM / UNTEN / EN BAS:
British oak chair, c. 1905

picturesque asymmetry to elevations. Unlike their Continental contemporaries, British architects were for the most part concerned with the arrangement and planning of domestic buildings rather than with public architecture or large-scale city plans.

The ascendancy of English domestic architecture in the late 19th and early 20th century paralleled the rise of the professional classes and the success of manufacturing entrepreneurs, the majority of whom desired spacious residences that also provided the charm and comfort of a "home". These grand, mostly country houses often required a large staff of domestic servants, gardeners and stable hands for their day-to-day running – extravagances that could be afforded due to low taxation and a relatively plentiful supply of cheap labour. Many such houses were inspired by the granges of medieval monasteries and featured large central halls. The revivalism that emerged in the 19th century – first Neo-Classicism and later Gothic – continued into the early 20th century and resulted in mainstream manufacturers producing a quantity of Elizabethan, Jacobean and Georgian style furnishings. Adherents of the New Art movement disparaged this backward-looking ten-

dency and concurred with C. H. B. Quennell that a "man in motor outfit, or arrayed as an aviator, is, to say the least of it, utterly incongruous in a mock Gothic hall". The electrically powered 20th century posed a different set of needs and concerns than the steam-powered 19th century, and designers and architects were now confronted with new building materials such as steel and concrete, which offered the potential of new constructional techniques.

By the early 1900s it was realised that, while William Morris's rejection of the machine was economically unsustainable, mechanised production should only be used for appropriate tasks and should not be employed to imitate handcraft. It was also widely acknowledged that architects should remain truthful to the modern materials now available and that these would eventually herald a new style. During the decade spanning 1900 to 1910, the demand for "better constructed and more artistic homes" spread across Europe; greater emphasis was placed on domestic planning, with the design of gardens often forming an important element of integrated schemes. Throughout this period the avant-garde mainly executed high quality designs and buildings for a select number of wealthy patrons, and it was not until the later 1910s that its promotion of reformed design began to be felt more widely.

In Britain, forward-looking designers and architects such as Charles Rennie Mackintosh had to battle against the inherent conservatism of mainstream taste, and often found that their designs were better received on the Continent than at home. The poorly resourced art schools in Britain also showed a total lack of understanding of industrial manufacture and were completely out of touch in their continued pursuit of craft. This "dearth of ideas" in Britain allowed the Continental avant-garde to assume the leadership of the New Movement or Jugendstil ("youth style"), as it became known in Germany. On the Continent, the applied arts were actively encouraged through state sponsorship, and Imperial Schools of Arts and Crafts were widely established in Germany – for example in Dresden, Munich, Darmstadt and Weimar. The New Movement also inspired the ahistorical Art Nouveau style emanating from Brussels, Nancy and Paris.

## Simplicity, Functionalism & Nationalism

By 1913 architecture was generally becoming less formal and pretentious, and there was a greater emphasis on massing, texture and colour. Better transportation systems increased the size of suburbs which, unlike earlier garden city plans, sprawled outwards in an uncontained way threatening rural areas. The growth of the suburbs with their plethora of small-sized homes meant that architects had to focus on better and more efficient internal planning. Functional concerns were now of paramount importance; space-saving fitted cupboards, for example, becoming more common. The drive for simplicity over ostentation meant that gardens, too, became less formal, with Gertrude Jeckyll's more naturalistic style of planting becoming highly fashionable. The naturalness and modesty of the "cottage ideal" captured the imagination of both the design community and the general public alike, while Sydney Jones in *Decorative Art* urged for such dwellings to "present one harmonious whole".

Although the new simplicity was primarily driven by function, the design and architecture of the years leading up to the First World War were marked not only by distinct national characteristics but also by intense regionalism.

Thus, within England, contemporary architecture in the Cotswolds differed significantly from that in Hampshire or Norfolk, for example, owing to different building traditions and local materials. German architecture displayed similar geographical variation, with cities such as Dresden, Munich, Darmstadt, Weimar and Hagen all trying to assert their own artistic autonomy. This regionalism was rooted in the belief that vernacularism, rather than technological progress, should underpin the new architecture: buildings should be in harmony with their surroundings, whether in an urban or countryside setting. This question of site suitability, however, was later discarded by proponents of the International Style in their pursuit of universalism.

## Healthy Living and Social Change

The home and its crucial relationship to health and hygiene prompted different ways of living during the early 20th century. In the late 1910s, for example, there was a vogue for open-air sleeping in loggias and on balconies, it being believed that this was beneficial to health. This interest in more healthful living increased after the First World War and became a primary concern of the Modern Movement during the 1920s and 1930s.

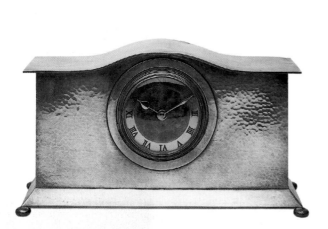

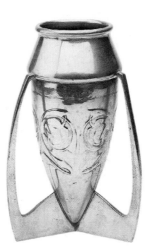

The First World War truly affected "every sphere of human activity", including the building of new homes. It left a chronic housing shortage – a government report of 1917 calculated that Britain needed half a million new homes for working-class people and those of small means. The situation was exacerbated by the demographic changes wrought by the four-year conflict: the "lost generation" of

soldiers who had not returned from the Front meant that there was a larger percentage of single women. These women by necessity had to work, which in turn led to greater female emancipation. The rigid class structures of the 19th century were also eroded as women from the aristocracy married beneath them, through a lack of men within their own peer group. At the same time, the servant class almost became a thing of the past, as many of the men returning from the war decided to become small shop owners, mechanics or factory workers rather than to re-enter domestic service. The ensuing increase in the number of smaller, low-income households meant that social housing was now a major national priority.

Although there was a desperate need for new homes, the war had also left a chronic shortage of materials. This meant that the hitherto theoretical advances in architecture and design could not be fully realized in practice until the following decade. At this stage concrete was a new, expensive and relatively untried material and its practicality for external walls had still not been fully ascertained. Indeed, it was not until the late 1920s and 1930s that concrete became widely used by avant-garde architects.

Even as commentators in the *Decorative Art* yearbooks of the late 1910s continued to urge for artistic quality in the design of homes, it was evident that the key to affording the mass housing so desperately needed was the use of new industrial materials and construction techniques. While standardisation was seen by proponents of the Modern Movement as a means of achieving the quantity of housing required, it was also seen as a "degradation" of individual creative expression by others. All concurred, however, that reconstruction would require a welding of art and industry if it were to truly benefit society. This synthesis between the arts and mechanisation found perhaps its greatest expression in the establishment of the Staatliches Bauhaus in Weimar in 1919 – an institution that fundamentally changed the course of design and gave concrete form to the principles of the Modern Movement. The devastation of the First World War had ensured that society was irreversibly transformed and that the objectives of design and architecture were altered beyond recognition – the social impetus of design was now firmly on the agenda.

# EINLEITUNG
## DIE 1900er UND 1910er JAHRE

### Die Moral der Neuen Kunst

Die Architektur und das Design des frühen 20. Jahrhunderts waren von einem neuen moralischen Empfinden durchdrungen, das sich aus den Reformansätzen von Designern wie William Morris und John Ruskin entwickelt hatte. Diese Designer, die sich zu einer Reformbewegung vereinigt hatten, wandten sich gegen den überladenen Dekorationsstil des viktorianischen Zeitalters und suchten nach einem neuen Ansatz, der Schönheit mit Nützlichkeit verbinden sollte. Seit Beginn ihres Erscheinens im Jahre 1906 dokumentierten die *Decorative Art*-Jahrbücher diese umwälzenden Veränderungen der tradierten Konventionen, indem sie vorzugsweise Entwürfe veröffentlichten, die sich durch ihre »Eignung für den Zweck« auszeichneten. Außerdem stellten sie für die britischen Designer eine lebenswichtige Verbindung zu ihren Kollegen auf dem europäischen Festland und in Amerika her, die die fortschrittlichen Neuerungen durch die reichhaltigen Illustrationen in den Jahrbüchern verfolgen konnten.

Die *Decorative Art*-Jahrbücher berichteten in jährlichen Überblicken nicht nur über die aktuellen Trends in der Raumgestaltung und der Architektur, sondern versuchten auch, allgemeine Richtlinien für die Architektur oder das Interior Design zu entwickeln. Unter Berücksichtigung psychologischer und praktischer Gesichtspunkte formulierten sie die Grundanforderungen an das Haus, wobei besonderer Wert auf Hygiene, Licht und Farbe gelegt wurde, die die Gesundheit und das Wohlbefinden positiv beeinflussten. Die Leser wurden ermutigt, einen harmonischen Ausgleich zwischen Farbe und Form zu suchen, der weder zu überladen noch zu langweilig wirkte. Die Vorliebe der oberen Gesellschaftsschichten für antike Möbel führte in diesen Jahren in der Mittelschicht zu einer steigenden Nachfrage nach Möbelimitationen. Die Jahrbücher wandten sich entschieden gegen diesen Trend des »sklavischen Kopierens« und wiesen darauf hin, dass dies den Fortschritt behindere und eine »narkotische Wirkung auf die Industrie« ausübe.

Obwohl das Art nouveau sich ursprünglich in England durch die Reformansätze so fortschrittlicher Architekten und Designer wie C. F. A. Voysey entwickelt hatte, verbreiteten sich um die Jahrhundertwende unabhängig voneinander auch auf dem europäischen Festland Reformbewe-

LEFT PAGE / LINKE SEITE / PAGE DE GAUCHE:
Archibald Knox, *Cymric* clock for Liberty & Co., 1903
BOTTOM LEFT / UNTEN LINKS / EN BAS À GAUCHE:
Hugh Thackeray Turner, Glazed porcelain bowl, 1913
BOTTOM RIGHT / UNTEN RECHTS / EN BAS À DROITE:
William De Morgan, Red lustre vase, c. 1900

gungen, besonders in Deutschland und Österreich, die extravagante überladene Dekorationen durch einfache funktionale Formen ersetzten. 1907 wurde in München der Deutsche Werkbund gegründet, eine der ersten Bewegungen, die sich ausdrücklich darum bemühten, Kunsthandwerk und industrielle Produktion miteinander zu verbinden. In Großbritannien entstand erst acht Jahre später, im Jahr 1915, mit der Design & Industries Association eine entsprechende Institution, und dies spiegelte deutlich den Verlust der intellektuellen und wirtschaftlichen Führung an Kontinentaleuropa wider. Als Reformbewegung gegen den hässlichen Kommerzialismus des 19. Jahrhunderts entstanden, wurde das Art nouveau zu einem internationalen Phänomen. Schon 1907 verwendete *Decorative Art* die Bezeichnung »Modern Style«, um diesen weit verbreiteten neuen Stil zu beschreiben, der in seiner Ausrichtung antihistoristisch und durch einfache, klare Linien gekennzeichnet war. Die Moderne manifestierte sich in Großbritannien am ausgeprägtesten in der angewandten und dekorativen Kunst, auf dem europäischen Festland dagegen in privaten und öffentlichen Gebäuden, die häufig als stilistisch homogene »Gesamtkunstwerke« konzipiert wurden.

### Ländliche Ideale und moderne Realität

Im 19. Jahrhundert dominierte in Großbritannien eine eher malerische Architektur, die in Stil, Materialien und in ihren sonstigen Aspekten an die jeweilige Umgebung angepasst war. Obwohl dies die Blütezeit des englischen Landhausstils war, lobten Architekten und Kritiker die ländlichen Cottages auch wegen ihrer gemütlichen Einfachheit. Der Klassizismus wurde allgemein als ein Baustil betrachtet, der für nördliche Klimazonen nicht geeignet war, und *Decorative Art* lehnte ihn als »künstlich, kalt und prunksüchtig« ab. Sein ausdrucksloser Charakter wurde seiner Symmetrie zugeschrieben. Die Verwendung von Stuck für Marmorimitationen wurde als Vortäuschung falscher Tatsachen besonders missbilligt. Stattdessen forderte man die Architekten auf, Baumaterialien aus der näheren Umgebung zu verwenden. Die Innenaufteilung sollte die äußere Form des Gebäudes bestimmen. Dies wiederum würde, so hoffte man, malerische asymmetrische Bauwerke hervorbringen. Im Gegensatz zu ihren Kollegen auf dem europäischen Festland, befassten sich die Architekten in England hauptsächlich mit der Ausstattung und Pla-

nung von Privathäusern und kaum mit öffentlichen Gebäuden oder übergreifender Stadtplanung.

Der Aufstieg der englischen Landhausarchitektur im ausgehenden 19. und frühen 20. Jahrhundert verlief parallel zur Entwicklung der sich neu formierenden höheren Berufsstände und zum Erfolg der industriellen Unternehmerklasse, die in geräumigen Landsitzen den Charme und Komfort eines »Heims« miteinander verband. Die Mehrzahl dieser Häuser konnte nur mit zahlreichen Hausangestellten, Gärtnern und Stallpersonal bewirtschaftet werden, ein extravaganter Luxus, den man sich nur aufgrund der niedrigen Besteuerung und des großen Angebots an billigen Arbeitskräften leisten konnte. Viele dieser Landsitze waren von mittelalterlichen Klosteranlagen mit Wirtschaftsgebäuden inspiriert und hatten eine große zentrale Halle. Das Aufleben des Neoklassizismus und der Neogotik im 19. Jahrhundert wirkte bis ins frühe 20. Jahrhundert hinein und hatte zur Folge, dass die meisten Produzenten überwiegend Möbel im »Elisabethan«, »Jacobean« und »Georgian Style« herstellten. Die Verfechter der Moderne wandten sich von diesen rückwärtsgewandten Trends ab und stimmten C. H. B. Quennell zu, der der Meinung war, dass ein »sportlich gekleideter moderner Autofahrer oder Flieger ganz und gar nicht in eine gotische Halle passt«. Das Zeitalter elektrisch angetriebener Maschinen brachte ganz andere Bedürfnisse und Probleme mit sich als das Zeitalter der Dampfmaschinen im frühen 19. Jahrhundert,

und Designer und Architekten waren nun mit neuen, modernen Konstruktionstechniken konfrontiert.

Bereits im frühen 19. Jahrhundert setzte sich die Erkenntnis durch, dass William Morris' Widerstand gegen die Maschine wirtschaftlich nicht vertretbar und die Anwendung mechanisierter Produktionsverfahren für bestimmte Aufgaben gerechtfertigt war, wenn sie das Handwerk nicht imitierten. Es wurde allgemein darauf gedrungen, dass die Architekten die neuen, modernen Baumaterialien verwandten, und man hoffte, dass dies schließlich einen neuen Stil hervorbringen würde. In den ersten Jahren des 20. Jahrhunderts stieg in ganz Europa die Nachfrage nach »besser konstruierten und künstlerisch gestalteten Häusern«. Auf die Innenraumgestaltung wurde größerer Wert gelegt, und Gartenanlagen bildeten oft einen wichtigen integralen Bestandteil des Bauplans. In diesem Jahrzehnt verwirklichte die Avantgarde für eine kleine Elite wohlhabender Bauherren Entwürfe und Gebäude von hoher Qualität. Erst in den letzten Jahren des Jahrzehnts wurden die Reformansätze in der Architektur von einer breiten Öffentlichkeit wahrgenommen.

In Großbritannien mussten fortschrittliche Designer und Architekten wie Charles Rennie Mackintosh gegen den erstarrten konservativen Geschmack der Allgemeinheit kämpfen, und sie machten die Erfahrung, dass ihre Entwürfe auf dem europäischen Kontinent begeisterter aufgenommen wurden als im eigenen Land. Den schlecht aus-

gestatteten Kunstschulen Großbritanniens fehlte es an jeglichem Verständnis für industrielle Produktionsverfahren, und sie hatten mit ihrer traditionellen handwerklichen Herstellung den Anschluss an die Moderne verpasst. Der mangelnde Ideenreichtum in Großbritannien ermöglichte es der europäischen Avantgarde, die Führung im »Modern Style« oder Jugendstil, wie die Bewegung in Deutschland genannt wurde, zu übernehmen. Auf dem Kontinent wurde das Kunsthandwerk durch staatliche Förderung aktiv unterstützt, und überall in Deutschland wurden staatliche Kunsthandwerksschulen eingerichtet – in Dresden, München, Darmstadt und Weimar, um nur einige zu nennen. Der Jugendstil inspirierte auch das Art nouveau, das von Brüssel, Nancy und Paris ausging. In Österreich sprach man vom »Sezessionsstil«.

### Schlichtheit, Funktionalismus und Nationalismus

Um 1913 wurde die Architektur zunehmend weniger formal und prunkvoll. Das Augenmerk lag nun auf Volumen, Textur und Farbe. Der Ausbau der Verkehrssysteme führte zu einem Anwachsen der Vorstädte, die sich im Gegensatz zu den ehemaligen Gartenstadtplanungen ungezügelt über die Stadtgrenzen hinweg ausbreiteten und zu einer Bedrohung für die angrenzenden ländlichen Gebiete wurden. Das Anwachsen der Vorstädte mit ihren zahllosen Einfamilienhäusern hatte zur Folge, dass die Architekten sich ver-

stärkt mit einer besseren und effizienteren Planung der Innenausstattung befassen mussten. Funktionale Gesichtspunkte gewannen Priorität, und raumsparende Einbauschränke wurden zum Allgemeingut. Mit dem Bemühen um funktionale Schlichtheit anstelle extravaganter Prunksucht wurden auch die Gärten weniger formal, und Gertrude Jeckylls »naturnahe« Gartenkultur kam in Mode. Die bescheidene Natürlichkeit des »Cottage«-Ideals bestimmte noch immer die Vorstellungen der Designer und der breiten Öffentlichkeit, während der Architekt Sidney Jones in *Decorative Art* dafür plädierte, dass Wohnungen »ein harmonisches Ganzes präsentieren«.

Obwohl die neue Schlichtheit hauptsächlich von der Funktionalität bestimmt wurde, waren Design und Architektur unmittelbar vor dem Ersten Weltkrieg nicht nur durch klare nationale Unterschiede, sondern auch durch einen ausgeprägten Regionalismus gekennzeichnet. In Großbritannien unterschied sich die zeitgenössische Architektur in den Cotswolds durch die traditionelle Bauweise und lokale Baumaterialien beispielsweise ganz deutlich von der in Hampshire oder Norfolk. Auch in Deutschland wies die Architektur regionale Unterschiede auf, und Zentren wie Dresden, München, Darmstadt, Weimar oder Hagen versuchten, künstlerische Autonomie zu etablieren und zu erhalten. Dieser Regionalismus wurzelte in der Überzeugung, dass sich die neue Architektur mehr auf der Basis regionaler Besonderheiten als aufgrund von techni-

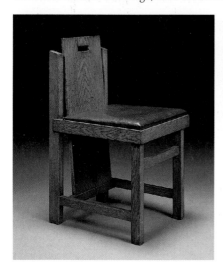

schem Fortschritt entwickeln sollte: Gebäude sollten harmonisch auf ihre Umgebung abgestimmt sein, ganz gleich, ob es sich um ein städtisches oder eine ländliches Ambiente handelte. Die Frage nach der Anpassung an den jeweiligen Standort wurde von den Verfechtern des Internationalen Stils in ihrem Streben nach Universalismus allerdings später aufgegeben.

### Gesundes Leben und sozialer Wandel

Das Entstehen der Moderne veränderte die traditionelle Lebensweise und führte im 20. Jahrhundert zu einer neuen Lebensgestaltung, bei der Gesundheit und Hygiene eine zentrale Bedeutung hatten. In den letzten Jahren des neuen Jahrzehnts wurde es zum Beispiel Mode, an der frischen Luft in Loggien oder auf Balkonen zu schlafen, da man dies für gesundheitsfördernd hielt. Das Interesse an einer gesünderen Lebensweise nahm nach dem Ersten Weltkrieg noch zu und entwickelte sich während der 20er und 30er Jahre zu einer primären Forderung der Moderne.

Der Erste Weltkrieg beeinflusste in der Tat »jeden Bereich menschlicher Aktivitäten«, einschließlich des Wohnungsbaus – die Kriegsverwüstungen hatten zu einem chronischen Wohnungsmangel in Europa geführt. Ein Regierungsbericht des Jahres 1917 stellte fest, dass in Großbritannien eine halbe Million neuer Wohnungen für Arbeiter und Geringverdienende benötigt wurden. Die demographischen Veränderungen als Folge des vierjährigen Krieges verschärften die Situation weiter: Die »verlorene Generation« von Soldaten, die an der Front gefallen war, hinterließ einen hohen Anteil unverheirateter Frauen, die in den Arbeitsprozess eingegliedert werden mussten, und dies führte zu einer verstärkten Emanzipation der Frauen. Das starre Klassensystem des 19. Jahrhunderts wurde auch dadurch aufgeweicht, dass Frauen aus der Aristokratie in gesellschaftlich niedrigere Schichten heirateten, da es weniger Männer in ihrer sozialen Schicht gab. Gleichzeitig verschwand die Klasse der Dienstboten fast vollständig, denn viele der aus dem Krieg zurückgekehrten Männer gründeten kleine Geschäfte, Werkstätten oder Betriebe, anstatt wieder eine Stellung als Hausbedienstete anzunehmen. Die daraus resultierende Zunahme kleiner Haushalte mit niedrigem Einkommen hatte zur Folge, dass sozialer Wohnungsbau zunehmend an Bedeutung gewann.

Mit der großen Wohnungsnot ging ein chronischer Mangel an Baumaterialien einher, sodass die bisher erreichten theoretischen Fortschritte in der Architektur und im Design in der Praxis erst im folgenden Jahrzehnt realisiert werden konnten. Beton war damals ein neues teures Baumaterial, für dessen Verwendung wenig Erfahrung bestand und dessen praktische Anwendung bei Außenmauern noch nicht gänzlich erprobt war. Es dauerte noch bis in die späten 20er und frühen 30er Jahre, bis Beton von den Architekten der Avantgarde allgemein verwendet wurde.

Auch wenn sich die Kommentatoren in den *Decorative Art*-Jahrbüchern der letzten Jahre des ersten Jahrzehnts weiterhin für eine hohe künstlerische Qualität im Wohnungsdesign einsetzten, war nicht zu übersehen, dass die Lösung für den dringend notwendigen Bau von Massenwohnungen in der Verwendung neuer industrieller Baumaterialien und Konstruktionstechniken lag. Während die Verfechter der Moderne in der Standardisierung ein Mittel zur Befriedigung des Wohnbedarfs sahen, wurde diese von anderen als »Degradierung« des individuellen kreativen Ausdrucks abgelehnt. In einem aber waren sich alle einig: Der Wiederaufbau konnte nur durch ein Zusammenwirken von Kunst und Industrie realisiert werden, wenn die Gesellschaft nachhaltig davon profitieren sollte. Diese Synthese von Kunst und Industrie fand im Jahre 1919 ihren prägnantesten Ausdruck in der Gründung des staatlichen Bauhauses in Weimar – einer Institution, die Architektur und Design grundlegend verändern sollte und den Prinzipien der Moderne konkrete Formen verlieh. Der Erste Weltkrieg hatte zu irreversiblen Veränderungen in der Gesellschaftsstruktur geführt und die Zielsetzungen von Design und Architektur radikal verändert – auch die sozialen Aufgaben des Designs wurden jetzt widerspruchslos anerkannt.

# INTRODUCTION
## LES ANNÉES 1900 ET 1910

### Le nouvel art moral

L'architecture et le design des premières années du 20e siècle furent imprégnés d'une nouvelle sensibilité morale issue des enseignements de réformateurs tels que William Morris et John Ruskin. Rejetant l'ornementation chargée du style « High Victorian », les créateurs qui rejoignirent ce nouveau courant suivaient une démarche plus réfléchie en grande partie fondée sur le concept de l'utile dans le beau. Dès leur apparition en 1906, les annuaires de *Decorative Art* reflétèrent ce changement de cap en mettant en avant des créations faisant preuve d'une « adéquation aux objectifs visés ». Ils assurèrent également un lien crucial entre les créateurs britanniques et leurs confrères du reste de l'Europe et des Etats-Unis. Chacun pouvait ainsi suivre le travail des autres grâce aux nombreuses illustrations présentant les nouveautés.

*Decorative Art* ne se contentait pas de rendre compte chaque année des dernières tendances en matière de bâtiments et d'ameublement mais cherchait également à instaurer en quelque sorte des principes directeurs pour l'architecture et la décoration d'intérieur. Les besoins d'une maison y étaient évalués d'un point de vue psychologique tout comme physique. On attachait un soin particulier à l'hygiène, l'éclairage et la couleur, trois domaines considérés comme influant sur la santé et le bien-être. Les lecteurs étaient incités à rechercher un équilibre harmonieux entre la couleur et la forme, qui ne devaient être ni trop exubérantes ni trop ternes. Au cours de cette période, l'engouement des classes les plus riches pour les antiquités déclencha une forte demande de reproductions de meubles anciens de la part des moins aisés. Les annuaires déploraient cette mode du « copiage servile », la décrivant comme une insulte au progrès et dénonçant son « effet soporifique sur les arts décoratifs ».

Bien que le « nouvel art » ait d'abord vu le jour en Grande-Bretagne grâce à des architectes et créateurs progressistes tels que C. F. A. Voysey, ce mouvement réformiste se développa de manière indépendante dans le reste de l'Europe dès le début du siècle. En Allemagne et en Autriche, notamment, les extravagances décoratives cédèrent progressivement la place à des formes plus simples et fonctionnelles. En 1907, le *Deutscher Werkbund* fut fondé à Munich. Ce fut l'une des premières organisations à se consacrer spécifiquement à la réconciliation entre la création artistique et la production industrielle. La Grande-Bretagne dut attendre huit ans avant d'avoir une institution équivalente, à savoir la *Design & Industries Association,* fondée en 1915 et reflet parlant du terrain philosophique et économique qui était progressivement accaparé par le reste de l'Europe. Présenté d'emblée comme une rébellion contre la laideur de la commercialisation du 19e siècle, le nouvel art devint rapidement un phénomène international. Le terme de « mouvement moderne » fut employé dès 1907 dans les annuaires de *Decorative Art* pour décrire ce nouveau style très répandu, qui rejetait l'historicisme et se caractérisait par le recours à des lignes simples et dépouillées. En Grande-Bretagne, il se manifestait surtout dans les arts décoratifs et appliqués. Dans le reste de l'Europe, il s'exprimait dans les bâtiments publics et privés, souvent conçus comme un *Gesamtkunstwerk* (« œuvre d'art totale »).

### Idées rurales et réalités modernes

Dans les années 1900, l'architecture britannique était assez portée sur le pittoresque et plutôt respectueuse du caractère, des matériaux et de l'aspect du paysage environnant. Si la grande demeure de campagne anglaise était à son apogée, les architectes et les critiques louaient également les vertus du « cottage » pour sa charmante simplicité. Le classicisme était généralement considéré comme inadapté aux climats nordiques et décrit dans *Decorative Art* comme « artificiel, froid et pompeux », sa symétrie étant assimilée à un manque de personnalité. Le recours au stuc pour imiter le marbre était particulièrement mal vu, car trompeur. A la place, on encourageait les architectes à utiliser des matériaux de la région et à laisser les plans intérieurs leur dicter l'aspect des façades. Cela devait, espérait-on, donner aux étages une asymétrie pittoresque. Contrairement à leurs confrères du continent européen, les architectes britanniques s'intéressaient surtout à l'agencement et aux projets de maisons particulières plutôt qu'aux bâtiments publics ou aux projets d'urbanisme à grande échelle.

L'ascendance de la maison particulière à la fin du 19e et au début du 20e siècle reflétait la montée en puissance des professions libérales et la réussite des entrepreneurs qui, pour la plupart, désiraient des résidences spacieuses qui aient également tout le charme et le confort d'un foyer. Ces vastes demeures, le plus souvent situées à la campagne, devaient être entretenues par un personnel nombreux –

domestiques, jardiniers et palefreniers – un luxe qui était encore abordable grâce à une fiscalité faible et une main d'œuvre relativement abondante et bon marché. Beaucoup s'inspiraient de manoirs et de monastères médiévaux et comportaient un vaste hall central. Le retour à des styles antérieurs, qui avait commencé au 19$^e$ siècle avec le néo-classicisme et le néogothique, perdura au début du 20$^e$ siècle. Les manufactures représentant le courant dominant produisirent en grande quantité des meubles inspirés des époques élisabéthaine, jacobéenne et georgienne. Les défenseurs du nouvel art s'insurgèrent contre cette tendance à retourner dans le passé et convenaient, avec C. H. B. Quennell, qu'un homme « en tenue d'automobiliste ou d'aviateur paraissait pour le moins déplacé dans un salon en faux gothique ». L'énergie électrique impliquait également d'autres besoins et préoccupations que la vapeur du 19$^e$ siècle. Les architectes et les designers disposaient désormais de nouveaux matériaux tels que l'acier et le béton qui offraient le potentiel de nouvelles techniques de construction.

Au début des années 1900, on estima que si le rejet par William Morris de la machine n'était pas viable sur le plan économique, la production mécanisée devait se limiter à certaines tâches et ne pas chercher à imiter l'artisanat. Il fut également communément admis que les architectes devaient rester fidèles aux matériaux modernes et que ces derniers finiraient par donner lieu à un nouveau style. Entre 1900 et 1910, la demande pour des « maisons mieux construites et plus artistiques » se répandit dans toute l'Europe. L'accent fut davantage mis sur les projets privés, les jardins aménagés constituant souvent un élément important du plan d'ensemble. Tout au long de cette période, l'avant-garde se concentra principalement sur des bâtiments et des créations d'une haute qualité pour un cercle restreint de riches commanditaires. Il fallut attendre la fin des années 1910 pour que le nouveau design se fasse sentir d'une manière plus générale.

En Grande-Bretagne, les créateurs et les architectes innovateurs tels que Charles Rennie Mackintosh durent

lutter contre le conservatisme inhérent du grand public. Leur travail était souvent mieux accueilli dans le reste de l'Europe que chez eux. Les écoles d'art britanniques, mal équipées, se montrèrent incapables d'assimiler les ressources de la fabrication industrielle et produisaient un artisanat totalement décalé. Cette «pénurie d'idées» permit à l'avant-garde d'autres pays européens de prendre la tête du nouveau mouvement, ou Jugendstil («le style de la jeunesse») tel qu'il était connu en Allemagne. A l'extérieur de la Grande-Bretagne, les arts appliqués étaient activement subventionnés par l'État. En Allemagne, les Ecoles d'Arts Impériales étaient bien établies, notamment à Dresde, Munich, Darmstadt ou Weimar. Le nouveau mouvement inspira également l'Art nouveau anti-historiciste qui émergeait à Bruxelles, Nancy et Paris.

## Simplicité, fonctionnalisme et nationalisme

Vers 1913, l'architecture se fit généralement moins formelle et prétentieuse. L'accent était davantage mis sur les volumes, les textures et les couleurs. L'amélioration des moyens de transports fit augmenter la taille des banlieues qui, contrairement aux plans antérieurs des villes concentrées autour de leurs jardins, s'étalaient vers l'extérieur d'une manière incontrôlée, menaçant les zones rurales. La croissance des banlieues avec leur pléthore de petites maisons força les architectes à se concentrer plus efficacement sur les plans intérieurs afin de les rendre mieux adaptés. Les préoccupations fonctionnelles étaient désormais d'une importance capitale, impliquant par exemple de plus en plus communément la conception de placards intégrés pour gagner de la place. La simplicité l'emportait sur l'ostentation. Même les jardins devinrent moins formels, les créations de la paysagiste naturaliste Gertrude Jeckyll devenant très à la mode. Le naturel et la simplicité du «cottage idéal» saisirent l'imagination à la fois des créateurs et du grand public, tandis que, dans les pages de *Decorative Art*, Sydney Jones insistait pour que ces habitations «présentent un ensemble harmonieux».

Bien que cette nouvelle simplicité soit surtout motivée par le fonctionnalisme, le design et l'architecture des années qui précédèrent la Première Guerre mondiale furent marqués non seulement par des caractères nationaux distincts mais également par un régionalisme inten-

se. Ainsi, en Angleterre, l'architecture moderne du Costwolds différait considérablement de celle du Hampshire ou du Norfolk, par exemple, et cela à cause des différents types de bâtiments traditionnels et de matériaux locaux. L'architecture allemande présentait des variations géographiques similaires, avec des villes telles que Dresde, Munich, Darmstadt, Weimar ou Hagen cherchant toutes à affirmer leur individualité artistique. Ce régionalisme se fondait sur le principe selon lequel le caractère local, plutôt que le progrès technologique, devait inspirer la nouvelle architecture. Les bâtiments devaient être en harmonie avec leur environnement, en ville comme à la campagne. Toutefois, cette question de l'adéquation au site devait être rejetée plus tard par les chantres du style international dans leur quête d'universalisme.

## Hygiène de vie et changements sociaux

Au début du 20e siècle, la maison et sa relation fondamentale à la santé et à l'hygiène engendrèrent de nouveaux modes de vie. A la fin des années 1910, par exemple, il devint très prisé de dormir au grand air sur les loggias et les balcons, car on pensait que c'était bon pour la santé. Cet intérêt pour une vie plus saine se renforça encore après la Grande Guerre pour devenir l'une des préoccupations majeures du mouvement moderne des années 1920 et 1930.

La Première Guerre mondiale affecta profondément «toutes les sphères de l'activité humaine», y compris le bâtiment. Elle entraîna une pénurie chronique de logements. En 1917, un rapport officiel estima que la Grande-Bretagne avait besoin d'un demi-million de nouveaux logements pour ses classes ouvrières et ses ménages à faibles revenus. Cette situation était encore exacerbée par les bouleversements démographiques dus aux quatre années de conflit: la «génération perdue» des soldats qui n'étaient pas rentrés du front fit considérablement augmenter le pourcentage de femmes célibataires. Ces dernières furent contraintes à travailler, ce qui entraîna une plus grande émancipation féminine. Les structures de classes rigides du 19e siècle furent également érodées par le grand nombre de femmes de la noblesse qui épousèrent des roturiers, faute de trouver des hommes de leur rang. Parallèlement, la catégorie sociale des domestiques tomba presque entièrement en désuétude: au retour du front, un grand nombre de domestiques préférèrent monter un petit commerce, devenir mécaniciens ou ouvriers d'usine plutôt que de reprendre du service chez leurs anciens patrons. Il s'ensuivit une augmentation des foyers plus petits et à plus faibles revenus, ce qui fit du logement social une véritable priorité nationale.

Parallèlement à un besoin urgent de nouveaux logements, la guerre entraîna également une pénurie chronique de matériaux de construction. Par conséquent, les progrès théoriques réalisés jusqu'ici en architecture et en design durent attendre la décennie suivante avant d'être réellement mis en pratique. A ce stade, le béton était encore nouveau et cher. Il avait été peu testé et la facilité de son utilisation pour les façades n'avait pas encore été complètement vérifiée. De fait, ce n'est qu'à la fin des années 20 et 30 que les architectes avant-gardistes se mirent à l'utiliser couramment.

Tandis que les commentateurs des annuaires de *Decorative Art* de la fin des années 1910 continuaient à encourager la qualité artistique dans la conception des maisons, il était évident que la meilleure solution pour fournir aux masses les logements qui leur faisaient si cruellement défaut était

d'exploiter les nouveaux matériaux industriels et les nouvelles techniques de construction. Si les tenants du modernisme voyaient dans la standardisation un moyen de satisfaire à la demande, d'autres la considéraient comme une « dégradation » de la créativité individuelle. Cependant, tous convenaient que la reconstruction devait réunir l'art et l'industrie pour que la société en profite réellement. Cette synthèse entre les arts et la mécanisation trouva sans doute sa meilleure expression dans la création du Staatliches Bauhaus de Weimar en 1919, une institution qui changea fondamentalement la tendance des arts appliqués et donna leur forme concrète aux principes du mouvement moderne. Les ravages de la Grande Guerre avaient irrémédiablement transformé la société et les objectifs du design et de l'architecture étaient altérés au-delà de toute reconnaissance. L'élan social du design était désormais résolument à l'ordre du jour.

architecture and interiors | Architektur und Interieurs | Architecture et intérieurs

BEDROOM WITH FURNITURE
IN PEAR WOOD

DESIGNED BY KARL BERTSCH, EXECUTED BY THE
WERKSTÄTTEN FÜR WOHNUNGSEINRICHTUNG, MUNICH

LIVING-ROOM WITH FURNITURE
IN WALNUT

DESIGNED BY KARL BERTSCH, EXECUTED BY THE
WERKSTÄTTEN FÜR WOHNUNGSEINRICHTUNG, MUNICH

LIVING-ROOM WITH FURNITURE
IN AFRICAN MAHOGANY

DESIGNED AND EXECUTED BY THE
LEIPZIGER KÜNSTLERBUND

ADDITION TO AN OLD BUILDING
AT LEIPZIG

RAYMUND BRACHMANN, ARCHITECT
(LEIPZIGER KÜNSTLERBUND)

LIVING-ROOM WITH FURNITURE
IN AFRICAN MAHOGANY

DESIGNED BY RAYMUND BRACHMANN AND
O. R. BOSSEN (LEIPZIGER KÜNSTLERBUND)

GARDEN ROOMS

WICKER FURNITURE BY JULIUS MOSLER
EMBROIDERIES BY GERTRUD LORENZ

FIREPLACE IN BEATEN COPPER WITH OAK
MANTELPIECE. DESIGNED BY A. HAROLD SMITH,
EXECUTED BY THE TEALE FIREPLACE CO.

DRAWING-ROOM FIREPLACE AT BRASTED, KENT.
MANTELPIECE IN ENGLISH WALNUT. DESIGNED
BY GEORGE WALTON, ARCHITECT

"THE HILL HOUSE," HELENSBURGH                    CHAS. R. MACKINTOSH, ARCHITECT

"THE HILL HOUSE," HELENSBURGH
CHAS. R. MACKINTOSH, ARCHITECT

THE DRAWING-ROOM AND BLUE BEDROOM AT
"THE HOUS'HILL," NITSHILL

CHAS. R. MACKINTOSH, ARCHITECT

THE DINING-ROOM AT "THE HOUS'HILL," NITSHILL    CHAS. R. MACKINTOSH, ARCHITECT

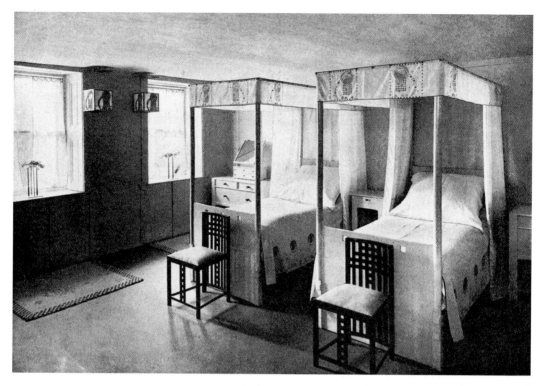

THE WHITE BEDROOM AT "THE HOUS'HILL," NITSHILL       CHAS. R. MACKINTOSH, ARCHITECT

DINING-ROOM IN OAK       DESIGNED AND EXECUTED BY MAPLE AND CO., LTD.

DINING-ROOM AT "ALMA HOUSE." GEORGE WALTON, ARCHITECT

ENTRANCE HALL AND DINING-ROOM AT
CHEYNE WALK, CHELSEA

C. R. ASHBEE, ARCHITECT. EXECUTED
BY THE GUILD OF HANDICRAFT, LTD.

BEDROOM WITH WALLS PANELLED
IN SILVER GREY WOOD.

DESIGNED AND EXECUTED BY J. S. HENRY, LTD.

DRAWING-ROOM WITH WALLS DECORATED WITH
APPLIQUÉ WORK IN UPPER PANELS AND IVORY ROMAN
SATIN IN LOWER.

DESIGNED AND EXECUTED BY J. S. HENRY, LTD.

DESIGN FOR A LIVING ROOM IN A BUNGALOW BY ALEX. GASCOYNE.
POLISHED WOOD FLOOR, COLOUR-WASHED CEILING, STENCILLED FRIEZE AND WHITE WOODWORK.

DESIGN FOR A DINING-ROOM BY H. D. SIMPSON.

LIVING ROOM IN A COUNTRY HOUSE DESIGNED BY
LEONARD F. WYBURD.

DRAWING-ROOM DESIGNED BY LEONARD F. WYBURD.

COTTAGE AND FARM-HOUSE                    A. JESSOP HARDWICK, F.R.I.B.A., ARCHITECT

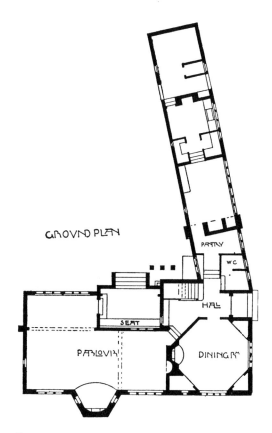

GROUND PLAN

PANTRY

WC

HALL

SEAT

PARLOUR

DINING Rᴹ

"THE HOMESTEAD," FRINTON-ON-SEA          C. F. A. VOYSEY, ARCHITECT

INTERIOR                     DESIGNED AND EXECUTED BY MAURICE DUFRÊNE

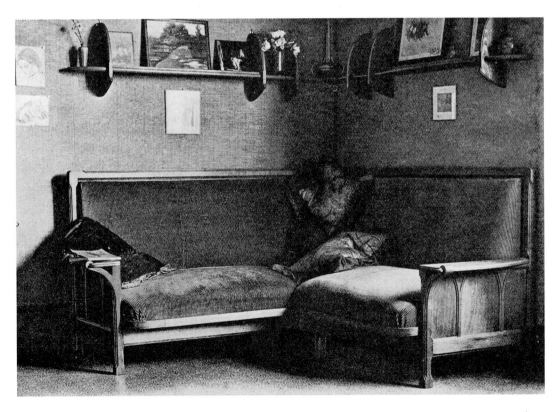

UPHOLSTERED SETTEE           DESIGNED AND EXECUTED BY MAURICE DUFRÊNE

INTERIOR DESIGNED AND EXECUTED
BY MAURICE DUFRÊNE

INTERIOR DESIGNED AND EXECUTED
BY THÉODORE LAMBERT

NURSERY DESIGNED AND EXECUTED BY SAUVAGE
AND SARRAZIN. FRIEZE BY FRANCIS JOURDAIN

HOUSE IN THE AVENUE MALAKOFF, PARIS
CHARLES PLUMET, ARCHITECT

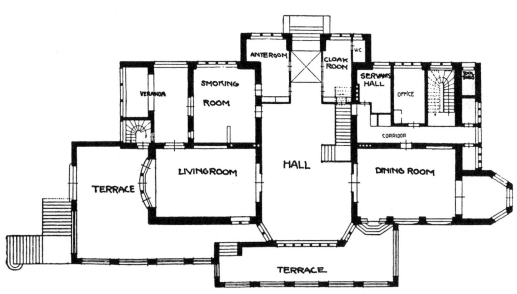

VILLA AT ZÜRICH. CURJEL
AND MOSER, ARCHITECTS

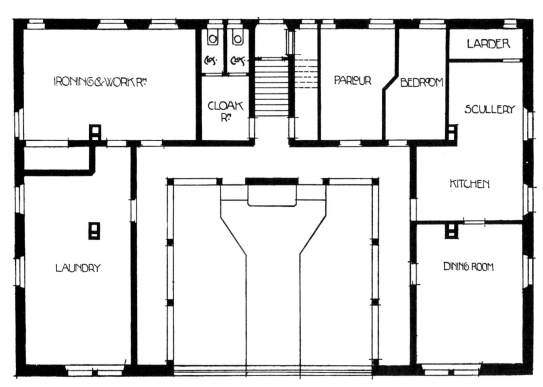

"MARIENHOF," HOME FOR GIRLS AT
BRAUNHARD, NEAR DARMSTADT

PROF. HEINRICH METZENDORF,
ARCHITECT

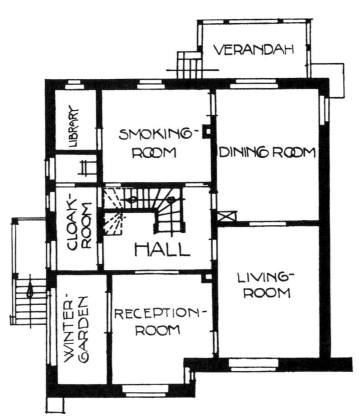

VILLA AT BENSHEIM                    PROF. HEINRICH METZENDORF, ARCHITECT

ARTIST'S STUDIO

HANS OFNER, ARCHITECT. EXECUTED
BY FRANZ MITTRINGER

CORNER OF A SMOKING-ROOM. PROF. RICHARD RIEMERSCHMID, ARCHITECT. EXECUTED BY THE DEUTSCHE WERKSTÄTTEN FÜR HANDWERKSKUNST, DRESDEN

CORNER OF A MUSIC ROOM. PROF. RICHARD RIEMERSCHMID, ARCHITECT. EXECUTED BY THE DEUTSCHE WERKSTÄTTEN FÜR HANDWERKSKUNST, DRESDEN

CORNER OF A LIVING-ROOM
PROF. ALBIN MÜLLER, ARCHITECT

DINING-ROOM FURNITURE DESIGNED BY PROF. RICHARD
RIEMERSCHMID, EXECUTED BY THE DEUTSCHE WERK-
STÄTTEN FÜR HANDWERKSKUNST, DRESDEN

LIVING-ROOM    PROF. RICHARD RIEMERSCHMID, ARCHITECT.    EXECUTED BY THE
DEUTSCHE WERKSTÄTTEN FÜR HANDWERKSKUNST, DRESDEN

DRAWING-ROOM FURNITURE    DESIGNED BY ARCH. RUDOLF WILLE

SITTING-ROOM DESIGNED AND EXECUTED BY LIBERTY & CO.

THE INNER HALL, LISVANE MANOR.
DESIGNED BY HERBERT D. RICHTER.

PARLOUR AT "THE HOMESTEAD," FRINTON-ON-SEA       C. F. A. VOYSEY, ARCHITECT

BEDROOM AT "THE HOMESTEAD," FRINTON-ON-SEA       C. F. A. VOYSEY, ARCHITECT

DINING-ROOM AT "THE HOMESTEAD,"      C. F. A. VOYSEY, ARCHITECT
FRINTON-ON-SEA

BOY'S BEDROOM    DESIGNED AND EXECUTED BY WARING AND GILLOW, LTD.

DRAWING-ROOM    DESIGNED BY LEONARD F. WYBURD

DINING ROOMS

DESIGNED BY PROF. OTTO GUSSMANN, EXECUTED BY THE
DEUTSCHE WERKSTÄTTEN FÜR HANDWERKSKUNST, DRESDEN

STUDY

DESIGNED BY PROF. RICHARD RIEMERSCHMID, EXECUTED BY THE
DEUTSCHE WERKSTÄTTEN FÜR HANDWERKSKUNST, DRESDEN

ENTRANCE HALL AT SUNNINGDALE DESIGN-
ED BY M. H. BAILLIE SCOTT, ARCHITECT

ENTRANCE HALL AND GALLERY
DESIGNED BY H. DAVIS RICHTER.

LIBRARY FIREPLACE          DESIGNED BY H. DAVIS RICHTER

DINING ROOM          DESIGNED BY PROF. RICHARD RIEMERSCHMID, EXECUTED BY THE
DEUTSCHE WERKSTÄTTEN FÜR HANDWERKSKUNST, DRESDEN

DINING-ROOM WITH SILVER-
GREY MAPLE FURNITURE

DESIGNED BY EDUARD WIGAND, EXECUTED
BY MICHAEL FODOR'S SUCCESSOR

DINING-ROOM WITH CARVED
OAK FURNITURE

DESIGNED BY EDUARD WIGAND
EXECUTED BY JOS. MOCSAI

ENTRANCE HALL                                      DESIGNED BY BÉLA LAJTA

ENTRANCE HALL WITH                DESIGNED BY GÉSA MARÓTI, EXECUTED BY
STAINED OAK FURNITURE            JOSEF KISS, GLASS MOSAIC BY MAX RÓTH

VILLA                                            HANS PRUTSCHER, ARCHITECT

DRAWING-ROOM.   CARL WITZMANN, ARCHITECT, EXECUTED BY DUMFORT AND TRÖSTER, AND EDUARD MUSIL

ENTRANCE HALL DESIGNED BY PROF. HOFFMANN
BENT-WOOD FURNITURE EXECUTED BY J. AND J. KOHN

TEA-ROOM. PROF. OTTO PRUTSCHER, ARCHITECT,
EXECUTED BY THE PRAG RUDNIKER KORBWAREN-
FABRIK, WINDOW BY CARL GEYLING'S ERBEN

DINING-ROOM IN ELM WOOD. ROBERT OERLEY,
ARCHITECT, EXECUTED BY ANTON POSPISCHIL,
CARPET BY J. GINZKEY

ENTRANCE HALL.  PROF. KOTĚRA, ARCHITECT

HOUSE AT HEILBRONN                    BEUTINGER AND STEINER, B.D.A., ARCHITECTS

BEDROOM                                        DESIGNED BY MAX HEIDRICH
                                               EXECUTED BY BERNARD STADLER

HOUSE AT HEILBRONN, BEUTINGER
AND STEINER, B.D.A., ARCHITECTS

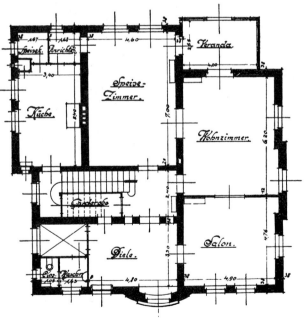

HOUSE  AT  ZEHLENDORF
PAUL MEBES,  ARCHITECT

HOUSE **AT** BREMEN, CARL EEG, B.D.A.,
AND ED. RUNGE, ARCHITECTS

KITCHEN AT BREMEN                    CARL EEG AND ED. RUNGE, ARCHITECTS

KITCHEN FURNITURE          DESIGNED BY CARL EEG AND ED. RUNGE, ARCHITECTS
                           EXECUTED BY F. H. SCHÄFER AND CO.

ENTRANCE AND LOGGIA OF RESIDENTIAL
FLATS AT CHARLOTTENBURG. ALBERT
GESSNER, ARCHITECT

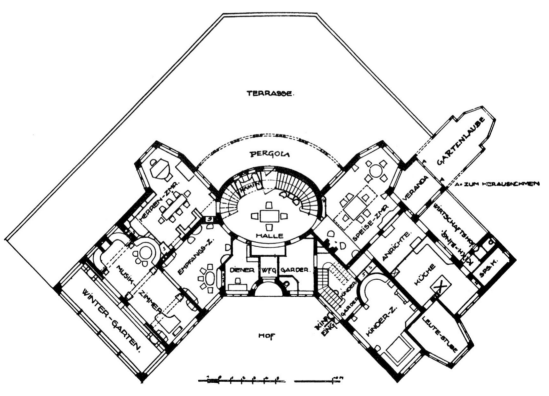

HOUSE AT NIKOLAS-SEE, DR.
HERMANN MUTHESIUS, ARCHITECT

HOUSE AT NIKOLAS-SEE                    DR. HERMANN MUTHESIUS, ARCHITECT

HOUSE AT WACHWITZ, NEAR DRESDEN          PROF. WILHELM KREIS, ARCHITECT

COTTAGE LIVING-ROOM AND
STUDY IN BIRCH WOOD

DESIGNED BY PROF. BRUNO PAUL, EXECUTED BY THE VEREINIGTE
WERKSTÄTTEN FÜR KUNST IM HANDWERK, MUNICH

BEDROOM, DESIGNED BY PROF. BRUNO PAUL
EXECUTED BY THE VEREINIGTE WERKSTÄTTEN
FÜR KUNST IM HANDWERK, MUNICH

BOUDOIR WITH FURNITURE     DESIGNED BY PROF. RICHARD RIEMERSCHMID
IN MAPLE WOOD     EXECUTED BY THE DEUTSCHE WERKSTÄTTEN FÜR HANDWERKSKUNST

CORNER OF A DRAWING-ROOM DESIGNED
AND EXECUTED BY LIBERTY AND CO., LTD.
CEILING BY G. P. BANKART.

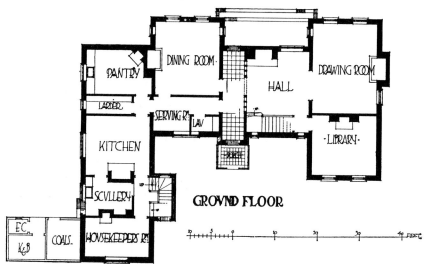

PANTRY

DINING ROOM·

DRAWING ROOM

LARDER

HALL

KITCHEN

SERVING R?· LAV

LIBRARY·

SCVLLERY

PORCH

GROVND FLOOR

EC.
K&B

COALS·

HOVSEKEEPER'S R?

"FOURACRE," WINCHFIELD,
HANTS.   ERNEST NEWTON,
F.R.I.B.A., ARCHITECT

HOUSE AT CHURCH-STRETTON, SALOP.
ERNEST NEWTON, F.R.I.B.A., ARCHITECT.

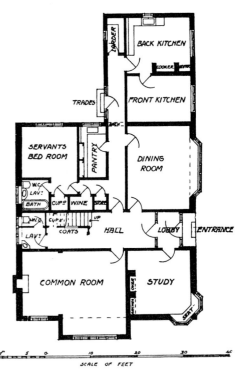

SCALE OF FEET

"THE NEW HOUSE," CHELMS-
FORD. C. H. B. QUENNELL,
F.R.I.B.A., ARCHITECT

COTTAGE AT BEACONSFIELD, BUCKS.
F. ROWNTREE, F.R.I.B.A., ARCHITECT

"WATERLOW COURT," HAMPSTEAD
M. H. BAILLIE SCOTT, ARCHITECT

"WERN FAWR," HARLECH
GEORGE WALTON, ARCHITECT

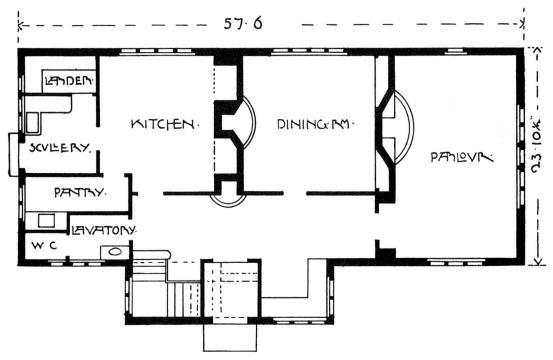

HOUSE AT PENN, BUCKS.
C. F. A. VOYSEY, ARCHITECT

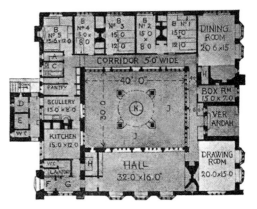

BUNGALOW NEAR BATH
C. F. A. VOYSEY, ARCHITECT

ENTRANCE HALL DESIGNED BY SHIRLEY B. WAIN-WRIGHT, EXECUTED BY FRANK COLLINSON AND CO.

"DUMBIEDYKES," KELVINSIDE, GLASGOW

JOHN EDNIE, ARCHITECT

STEPS AND DOORWAY AT "DUMBIEDYKES"

JOHN EDNIE, ARCHITECT

HOUSE AT NORTHWOOD        W. A. AICKMAN, F.R.I.B.A., ARCHITECT

"BRIARSIDE," EWELL, SURREY        W. A. AICKMAN, F.R.I.B.A., ARCHITECT

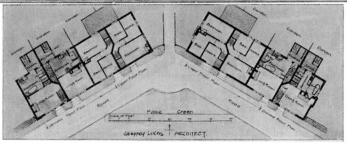

COTTAGES AT LETCHWORTH AND APSLEY GUISE,
BEDS. GEOFFRY LUCAS, A.R.I.B.A., ARCHITECT.

HOUSE AND GARDEN AT NEU-BABELSBERG
PROF. PETER BEHRENS, ARCHITECT

GARDENS AND GARDEN FURNITURE
DESIGNED BY PROF. KOLO MOSER

LIVING-ROOMS DESIGNED
BY PROF. JAN KOTĚRA

GARDEN-ROOM DESIGNED BY FREIHERR VON KRAUSS
EXECUTED BY A. POSPISCHIL. PAINTINGS BY O. GRILL

BEDROOM FURNITURE DESIGNED BY
PROF. JOSEF HOFFMANN, EXECUTED
BY THE WIENER WERKSTAETTE

THE IMPERIAL SCHOOL FOR STEEL-ENGRAVING, STEYR          A. RODLER, ARCHITECT

PAVILION AT THE HUNTING AND SPORTING EXHIBITION, VIENNA
DESIGNED BY PROF. OTTO PRUTSCHER, EXECUTED BY LUDWIG BIBER

ENTRANCE HALL DESIGNED BY PROF. OTTO PRUTSCHER
EXECUTED BY A. KNOBLOCHS NACHFOLGER

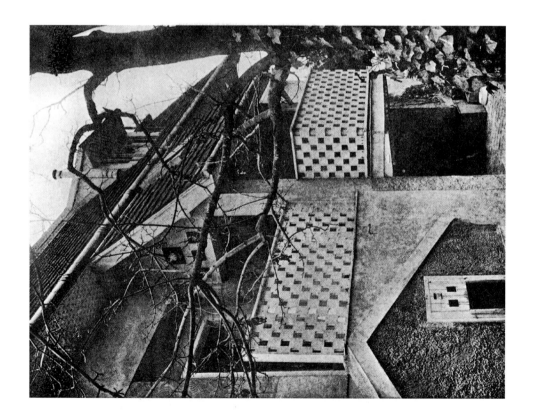

VERANDA AND DINING-ROOM OF A VILLA
DESIGNED BY JOSEF URBAN, ARCHITECT

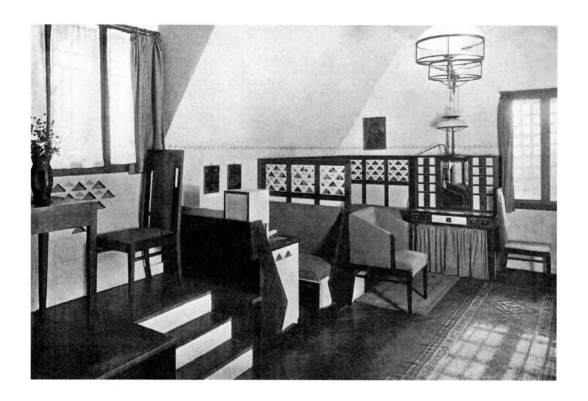

BEDROOM AND SITTING-ROOM                    DESIGNED BY JOSEF URBAN, ARCHITECT

BUFFET AND DRAWING-ROOM
FURNITURE

DESIGNED BY PROF. JOSEF HOFFMANN,
EXECUTED BY THE WIENER WERKSTAETTE

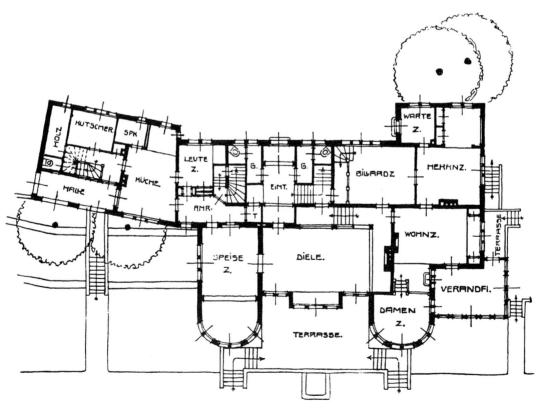

HOUSE AT DILLENBURG                    PROF. HUGO EBERHARDT, B.D.A., ARCHITECT

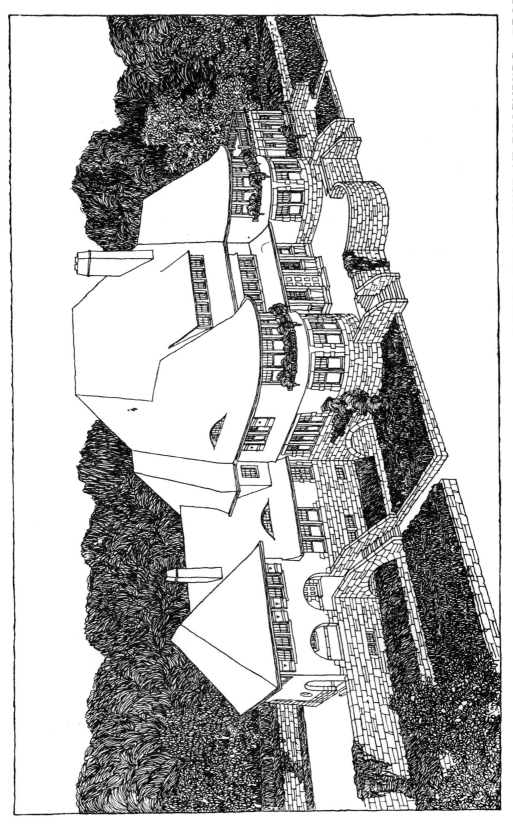

DESIGN FOR A HOUSE AT DILLENBURG. PROF.
HUGO EBERHARDT, B.D.A., ARCHITECT

HOUSE AT NEU-BABELSBERG
LUDWIG MIES, ARCHITECT

"THE GRANGE," PACKFIELD
ENTRANCE FRONT

R. SCOTT COCKRILL, A.R.I.B.A. ARCHITECT

"THE GRANGE," PACKFIELD
GARDEN FRONT

R. SCOTT COCKRILL, A.R.I.B.A., ARCHITECT

ADDITIONS TO SHIRENEWTON HALL,
CHEPSTOW. NORMAN EVILL, ARCHITECT.

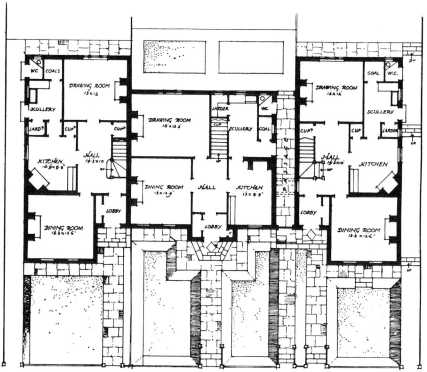

HOUSES AT WIMBLEDON
W. & E. HUNT, ARCHITECTS

HOUSE AT DURSLEY, GLOS.
P. MORLEY HORDER. F.R.I.B.A., ARCHITECT.

GARDEN HOUSE ON A SMALL LAKE, DESIGNED BY W. ARTHUR RIGG, A.R.I.B.A., EXECUTED BY JOHN RIGG AND SON

HOUSE AND GARDEN HOUSE
AT BREMEN. CARL EEG AND
EDUARD RUNGE, ARCHITECTS

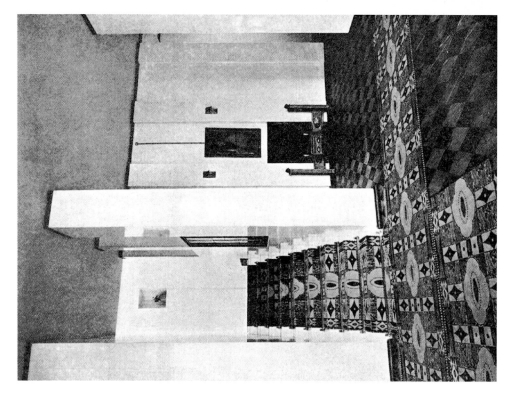

THE WATER-GARDEN AND STAIRCASE AT VILLA AST. PROF. JOSEF HOFFMANN ARCHITECT, EXECUTED BY THE WIENER WERKSTAETTE

DESIGN FOR A MUSIC-ROOM
BY FRANZ SCHWARZ, ARCHITECT.

RECEPTION ROOM AND
SMOKING-LOUNGE

DESIGNED BY PROF. OTTO PRUTSCHER, ARCHITECT
WINDOW OF SMOKING-LOUNGE BY H. VON ZWICKLE

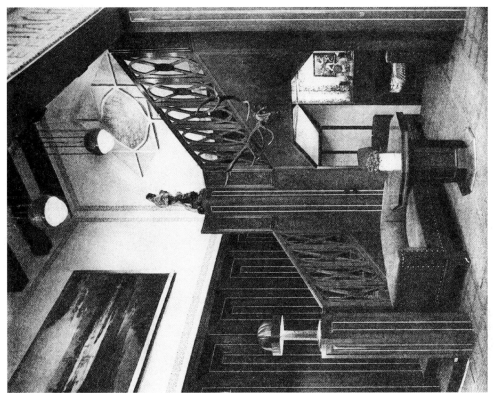

RECEPTION ROOM AND STAIRCASE DESIGNED BY PROF. OTTO PRUTSCHER, ARCHITECT

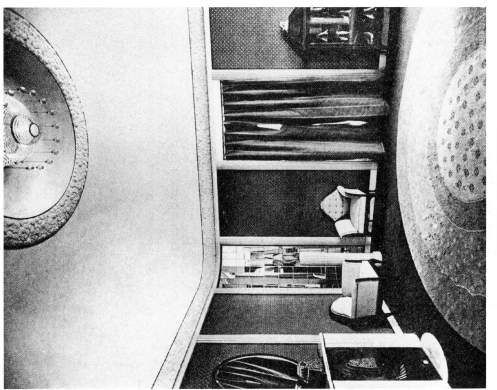

CLUB-HOUSE                                    RUNGE AND SCOTLAND, ARCHITECTS

DINING-ROOM                           DESIGNED BY PROF. RICHARD RIEMERSCHMID,
                                      ARCHITECT, EXECUTED BY THE DEUTSCHE WERK-
                                      STÄTTEN FÜR HANDWERKSKUNST, DRESDEN

DESIGN FOR A COUNTRY HOUSE
BY RUNGE AND SCOTLAND, ARCHITECTS.

HOUSE AT SCHAFFHAUSEN—ENTRANCE
DOORWAY AND SWIMMING BATH

CURJEL AND MOSER, ARCHITECTS

HOUSE AT SCHAFFHAUSEN—GARDEN
HOUSE AND SMOKING-ROOM

DESIGNED BY CURJEL AND MOSER, ARCHITECTS

HOUSE AT PINNER. R. A. BRIGGS AND BROWNING, ARCHITECTS.

PAIR OF COTTAGES AT LETCHWORTH                    R. F. JOHNSTON, ARCHITECT

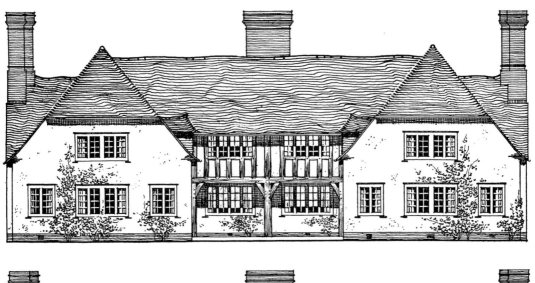

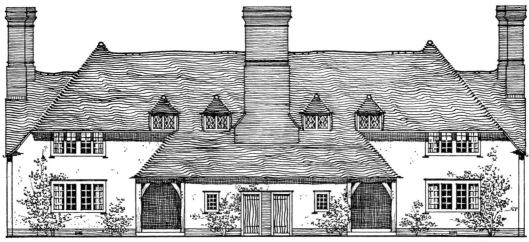

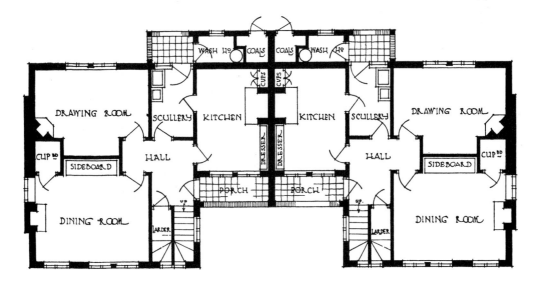

PAIR OF COTTAGES AT LETCHWORTH     R. F. JOHNSTON, ARCHITECT

"ST. BRIDGIDS," LETCHWORTH—THE GARDEN FRONT
AND LIVING-ROOM. PARKER AND UNWIN, ARCHITECTS

DRAWING-ROOM INGLE DESIGNED
BY JOHN EDNIE, ARCHITECT.

"UNDERSHAW," GUILDFORD—THE
ENTRANCE AND GARDEN FRONTS

M. H. BAILLIE SCOTT, ARCHITECT

"UNDERSHAW," GUILDFORD—THE HALL
BAY.  M. H. BAILLIE SCOTT, ARCHITECT

"UNDERSHAW," GUILDFORD
THE INNER HALL AND STUDY

M. H. BAILLIE SCOTT, ARCHITECT

"UNDERSHAW," GUILDFORD—THE GARDEN
FRONT.  M. H. BAILLIE SCOTT, ARCHITECT

DAY AND NIGHT NURSERIES DESIGNED
BY JÓZSEF VÁGÓ, ARCHITECT

"VILLA SCHIFFER," BUDAPEST
JÓZSEF VÁGÓ, ARCHITECT

ENTRANCE TO A THEATRE AT BUDAPEST
DESIGNED BY JÓZSEF VÁGÓ, ARCHITECT

ENTRANCE TO THE PETÖFI MUSEUM, BUDAPEST
DESIGNED BY JÓZSEF VÁGÓ, ARCHITECT

SITTING-ROOM                                   DESIGNED BY DR. JOSEF FRANK, ARCHITECT

VESTIBULE OF THE PEOPLE'S HALL, KÖNIGGRÄTZ        DESIGNED BY PROF. JAN KOTĚRA, ARCHITECT

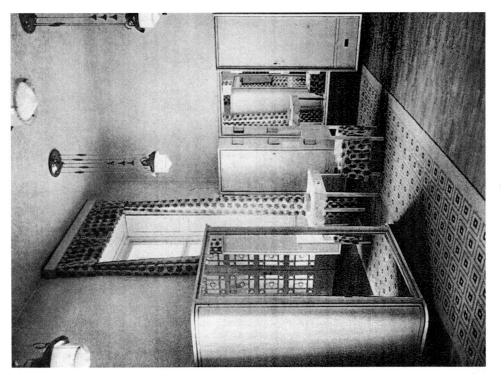

BEDROOM DESIGNED BY MAGDA MAÜTNER VON MARKHOF
EXECUTED BY WENZEL HOLLMANN

CORRIDOR AT VILLA AST, VIENNA
DESIGNED BY PROF. JOSEF HOFFMANN, ARCHITECT

"REIGEN"—RELIEF IN CHASED
COPPER AND ENAMEL

DESIGNED AND EXECUTED
BY EMIL MEIER

DINING-ROOM AT THE
HOTEL WIESLER, GRATZ

DESIGNED BY MARCEL KAMMERER, ARCHITECT
MOSAIC DESIGNED AND EXECUTED BY LEOPOLD
FORSTNER IN THE WIENER MOSAIK WERKSTAETTE

ANTEROOM DESIGNED BY KARL WITZMANN
ARCHITECT, EXECUTED BY LUDWIG SCHMIDT

ENTRANCE HALL AND STAIRCASE. DESIGNED
BY ALFRED ALTHERR. ARCHITECT

HOUSE NEAR ELBERFELD. ALFRED ALTHERR, ARCHITECT

WICKER FURNITURE                    DESIGNED AND EXECUTED BY DERICHS AND SAUERTEIG

SOFA FITMENT                        DESIGNED AND EXECUTED BY GUSTAV DORÉN

DRAWING-ROOM                    DESIGNED BY DR. HERMANN MUTHESIUS, ARCHITECT

DRAWING-ROOM                    DESIGNED BY DR. HERMANN MUTHESIUS, ARCHITECT

HOUSE AT RHEDE                                    DR. HERMANN MUTHESIUS, ARCHITECT

HOUSE AT RHEDE                                    DR HERMANN MUTHESIUS, ARCHITECT

GARDEN-HOUSE                    DESIGNED BY REINHOLD HOEMANN

HOUSE AT WITZENHAUSEN                    PROF. RICHARD RIEMERSCHMID, **ARCHITECT**
THE TERRACE

SITTING-ROOM AND BEDROOM DESIGNED BY PROF. RICHARD RIEMERSCHMID
EXECUTED BY THE DEUTSCHE WERKSTÄTTEN FÜR HANDWERKSKUNST, MUNICH AND DRESDEN-HELLERAU

DINING ROOM DESIGNED BY PROF. RICHARD RIEMERSCHMID, EXECUTED BY THE
DEUTSCHE WERKSTÄTTEN FÜR HANDWERKSKUNST, DRESDEN–HELLERAU

ENTRANCE HALL IN A COTTAGE
AT WITZENHAUSEN

DESIGNED BY PROF. RICHARD RIEMERSCHMID
EXECUTED BY THE DEUTSCHE WERKSTÄTTEN
FÜR HANDWERKSKUNST, DRESDEN-HELLERAU

ENTRANCE HALL AT ULM

DESIGNED BY PROF. RICHARD RIEMERSCHMID
EXECUTED BY THE DEUTSCHE WERKSTÄTTEN
FÜR HANDWERKSKUNST, MUNICH

HOUSE AT CLIMPING, SUSSEX                                        C. J. KAY. ARCHITECT

HOUSE AT PAGHAM, SUSSEX                                          C. J. KAY, ARCHITECT

PORTION OF A ROOM DESIGNED BY FRANK BRANGWYN, A.R.A.

"PLAS WERNFAWR," HARLECH—ORGAN-FRONT IN
ANCONA WALNUT, WITH CARVINGS DESIGNED
BY GEORGE WALTON, ARCHITECT

"PLAS WERNFAWR," HARLECH—THE LIBRARY
GEORGE WALTON, ARCHITECT

COTTAGE AT CHILWELL, NOTTS.—THE
LIVING-ROOM AND ENTRANCE FRONT

J. RIGBY POYSER, ARCHITECT

HOUSE AT WORPLESDON. LEONARD MARTIN, F.R.I.B.A., ARCHITECT

"THE CLOISTERS," REGENT'S PARK
THE ENTRANCE FRONT

M. H. BAILLIE SCOTT, ARCHITECT

"THE CLOISTERS," REGENT'S PARK
M. H. BAILLIE SCOTT, ARCHITECT

MANTELPIECE AND FIREPLACE
DESIGNED BY JESSIE M. KING.
EMBROIDERED PANELS WORKED
BY ÉLISE PRIOLEAU

"GARDEN CORNER," CHELSEA—THE DRAWING-ROOM. DESIGNED BY C. F. A. VOYSEY, ARCHITECT

"PLAS WERNFAWR," HARLECH—THE LIBRARY
GEORGE WALTON, ARCHITECT

"PLAS WERNFAWR," HARLECH—THE DINING-
ROOM.  GEORGE WALTON, ARCHITECT

DESIGN FOR A BILLIARD-ROOM
BY MURRAY ADAMS-ACTON

DESIGN FOR A LIVING-ROOM.   BY WILLIAM MACKINTOSH

ENTRANCE HALL        DESIGNED BY PROF. OTTO PRUTSCHER, FURNITURE EXECUTED BY L. MAYER-VILLACH

BEDROOM DESIGNED BY PROF. OTTO PRUTSCHER, ARCHITECT

VILLA BIENENFELD, BADEN.   PROF. OTTO PRUTSCHER, ARCHITECT

SALON IN BUDAPEST DESIGNED
BY JÓZSEF VÁGÓ, ARCHITECT

HALL IN BUDAPEST DESIGNED BY JÓZSEF VÁGÓ, ARCHITECT
WICKER FURNITURE DESIGNED BY PROF. JOSEF HOFFMANN

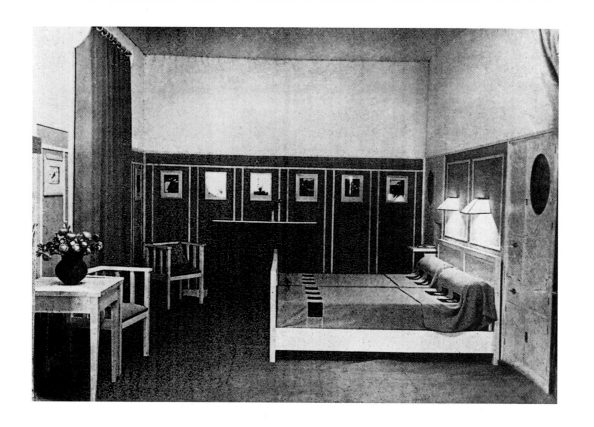

BEDROOM AND DINING-ROOM DESIGNED BY FRANCIS JOURDAIN, EXECUTED BY "LES ATELIERS MODERNES"

LIBRARY AND BEDROOM DESIGNED BY FRANCIS JOURDAIN, EXECUTED BY "LES ATELIERS MODERNES"

BEDROOM AND ENTRANCE HALL

DESIGNED BY ROB. MALLET-STEVENS
EXECUTED BY SCHNEIDERLIN

RECEPTION-ROOM                    DESIGNED AND EXECUTED BY JACQUES RUHLMANN

BATH-ROOM                         DESIGNED AND EXECUTED BY "MARTINE"

BOUDOIR DESIGNED AND EXECUTED
BY LOUIS MAJORELLE; DECORATIVE
PAINTING BY JACQUES MAJORELLE

DINING-ROOM DESIGNED AND EXECUTED
BY LOUIS MAJORELLE

HOUSE AT KÖNIGSTEIN (TAUNUS)                    PROF. HUGO EBERHARDT, ARCHITECT

DINING-ROOM INGLE                    DESIGNED BY PROF. HUGO EBERHARDT, ARCHITECT

Architekt Prof. H. Eberhardt

DESIGN FOR A HOUSE AT KÖNIGSTEIN (TAUNUS)
PROF. HUGO EBERHARDT, ARCHITECT

HOUSE AT DARMSTADT—ENTRANCE
FRONT AND DAY-NURSERY

PROF. ALBIN MÜLLER, ARCHITECT

HOUSE AT DARMSTADT                    PROF. ALBIN MÜLLER, ARCHITECT

HOUSE AT MAGDEBURG                    PROF. ALBIN MÜLLER, ARCHITECT

LIBRARY DESIGNED BY PROF. ADELBERT NIEMEYER
EXECUTED BY THE DEUTSCHE WERKSTÄTTEN FÜR
HANDWERSKUNST, MUNICH

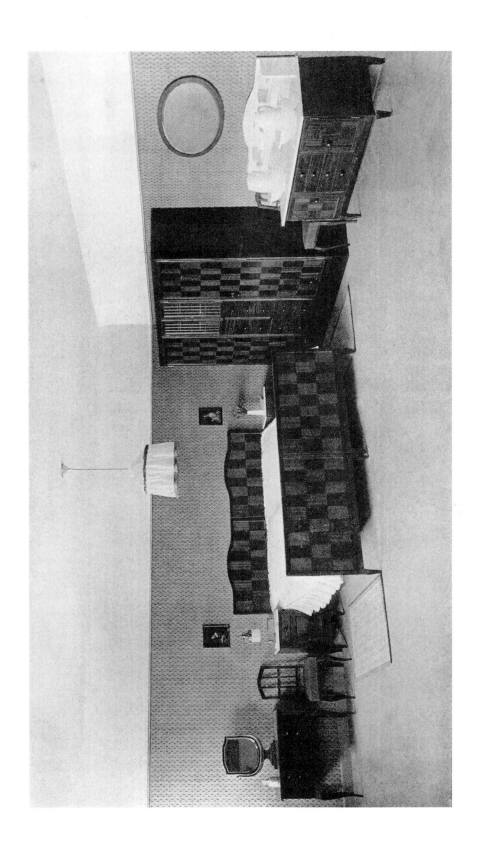

BEDROOM DESIGNED BY PROF. ADELBERT NIEMEYER, EXECUTED BY THE
DEUTSCHE WERKSTÄTTEN FÜR HANDWERKSKUNST, DRESDEN-HELLERAU

ENTRANCE HALL OF A COTTAGE                                DESIGNED BY ERNST HAIGER, ARCHITECT

DRAWING-ROOM                                DESIGNED BY PROF. BRUNO PAUL, EXECUTED BY THE VEREINIGTE
                                            WERKSTÄTTEN FÜR KUNST IM HANDWERK, BERLIN

DRAWING-ROOM FURNITURE DESIGNED BY PROF. RICHARD RIEMERSCHMID, EXECUTED BY THE DEUTSCHE WERKSTÄTTEN FÜR HANDWERKSKUNST, DRESDEN-HELLERAU

HOUSE NEAR FÜSSEN                                    PROF. RICHARD RIEMERSCHMID, ARCHITECT

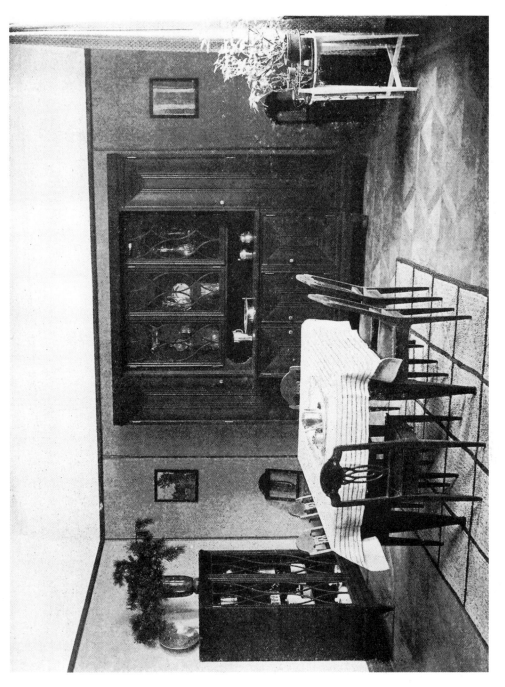

DINING-ROOM DESIGNED BY PROF. RICHARD RIEMERSCHMID, EXECUTED BY
THE DEUTSCHE WERKSTÄTTEN FÜR HANDWERKSKUNST, DRESDEN-HELLERAU

"ESSART," NEWBURY BERKS.—MAIN DOORWAY
O. P. MILNE, F.R.I.B.A., ARCHITECT

"THE PARSONAGE FARM," SHIPTON-UNDER-WYCHWOOD
O. P. MILNE, F.R.I.B.A., ARCHITECT

"THE PARSONAGE FARM," SHIPTON-UNDER-WYCHWOOD
SOUTH FRONT. O. P. MILNE, F.R.I.B.A., ARCHITECT

HALL DESIGNED FOR A COUNTRY
HOUSE. BY R. H. DESCHANEL.

INTERIORS OF COTTAGES AT ROMFORD          M. H. BAILLIE SCOTT, ARCHITECT

**COTTAGES** AT ROMFORD

M. H. BAILLIE SCOTT, ARCHITECT

**INTERIOR** OF A COTTAGE AT ROMFORD

M. H. BAILLIE SCOTT, ARCHITECT

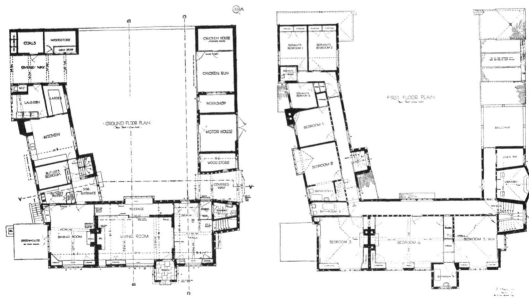

HOUSE AT SHORT HILLS, NEW JERSEY
M. H. BAILLIE SCOTT, ARCHITECT

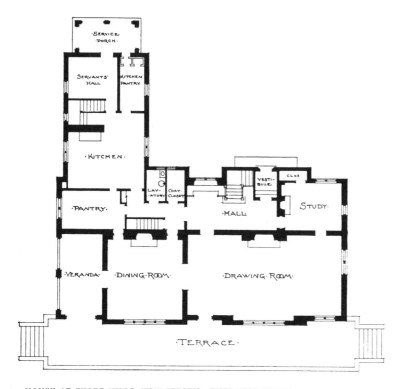

HOUSE AT SHORT HILLS, NEW JERSEY—ENTRANCE FRONT          ARTHUR C. NASH, ARCHITECT

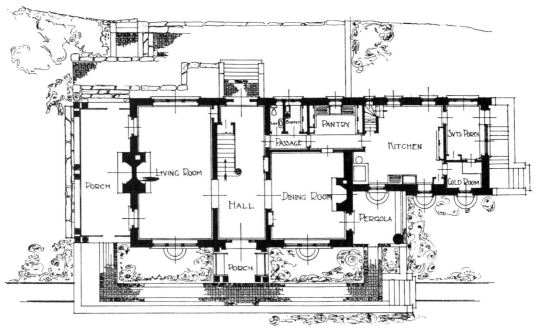

HOUSE AT GERMANTOWN, PENNSYLVANIA
DUHRING, OKIE AND ZIEGLER, ARCHITECTS

HOUSE AT GERMANTOWN, PENNSYLVANIA
DUHRING, OKIE AND ZIEGLER, ARCHITECTS

HOUSE AT GERMANTOWN, PENNSYLVANIA
DUHRING, OKIE AND ZIEGLER, ARCHITECTS

HOUSE AT GERMANTOWN, PENNSYLVANIA
DUHRING, OKIE AND ZIEGLER, ARCHITECTS

HOUSE AT RYE, NEW YORK—GARDEN FRONT
UPJOHN AND CONABLE, ARCHITECTS

HOUSE AT RYE, NEW YORK—ENTRANCE FRONT
UPJOHN AND CONABLE, ARCHITECTS

HOUSE NEAR WOKING—THE HALL
M. H. BAILLIE SCOTT, ARCHITECT

HOUSE NEAR WOKING. M. H. BAILLIE SCOTT, ARCHITECT

HOUSE AND GARDEN AT CANLEY
CORNER, NEAR COVENTRY. SYDNEY R.
JONES AND H. W. HOBBISS, ARCHITECTS

FIREPLACE AT CANLEY CORNER
NEAR COVENTRY.   SYDNEY R. JONES
AND H. W. HOBBISS, ARCHITECTS

GARDEN HOUSE AT WOOLLEY HALL
NEAR MAIDENHEAD. DESIGNED BY
THOS. H. MAWSON, HON. A.R.I.B.A.

"COMELY BANK," ENGLEFIELD GREEN, SURREY
H. S. GOODHART-RENDEL, ARCHITECT

HATLEY PARK, VICTORIA, B.C.

S. McCLURE, ARCHITECT

HATLEY PARK, VICTORIA, B.C.   S. McCLURE, ARCHITECT

HOUSE AT CALGARY

HODGSON AND BATES, ARCHITECTS

ENTRANCE GATEWAY AT TORONTO

J. M. LYLE, ARCHITECT

HOUSE AT PORT COLBORNE, ONT.—THE LIVING-ROOM
A. E. NICHOLSON, ARCHITECT

HOUSE AT HAMILTON

MILLS AND HUTTON, ARCHITECTS

HOUSE AT WINNIPEG                    JOHN D. ATCHISON, ARCHITECT

**PAIR OF** HOUSES AT MONTREAL                    E. AND W. S. MAXWELL, ARCHITECTS

"VILLA ARCADIA," JOHANNESBURG—THE GARDENS AND DRAWING-ROOM.     HERBERT BAKER, F.R.I.B.A., ARCHITECT

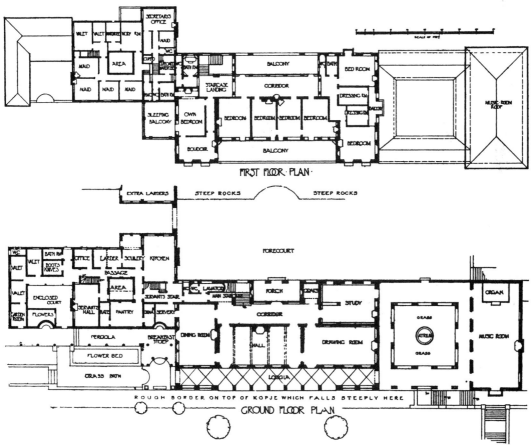

FIRST FLOOR PLAN

GROUND FLOOR PLAN

"VILLA ARCADIA," JOHANNESBURG          HERBERT BAKER, F.R.I.B.A., ARCHITECT

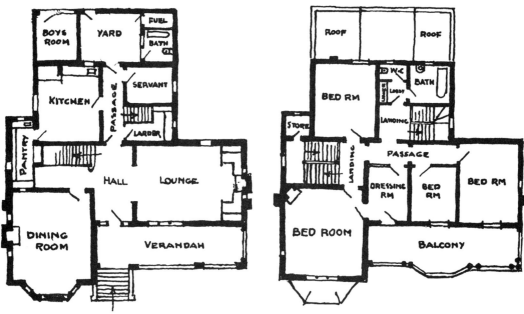

"CHARLEROI," SEA POINT, CAPE TOWN
LYON AND FALLON, ARCHITECTS

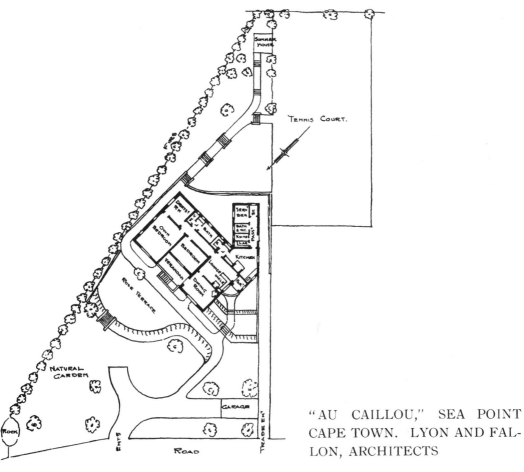

"AU CAILLOU," SEA POINT CAPE TOWN. LYON AND FAL-LON, ARCHITECTS

"CHEYNE," KENILWORTH, CAPE TOWN    A. AND W. REID, ARCHITECTS

THE PARSONAGE, MONTAGU    PARKER AND FORSYTH, ARCHITECTS

SEASIDE VILLA AT ST. JAMES, NEAR CAPE TOWN
W. J. DELBRIDGE, A.R.I.B.A., ARCHITECT

ENTRANCE PORCH OF NURSES' DORMITORY, SOMERSET HOSPITAL, CAPE TOWN
PARKER AND FORSYTH, ARCHITECTS

BUNGALOW AT DAYS BAY, NEW ZEALAND

BEERE AND GREENISH, ARCHITECTS

HOUSE OF ST. CLAIR, DUNEDIN
J. A. BURNSIDE, ARCHITECT
NEW ZEALAND

HOUSE AT PALMERSTON NORTH, NEW ZEALAND

F. DE J. CLERE AND SON, ARCHITECTS

HOUSE NEAR WELLINGTON, NEW ZEALAND

F. DE J. CLERE, F.R.I.B.A, ARCHITECT

BUNGALOW NEAR WELLINGTON, NEW ZEALAND

F. DE J. CLERE, F.R.I.B.A., ARCHITECT

"LANSDOWNE," MARLBOROUGH, NEW ZEALAND          W. HOULKER, ARCHITECT

BUNGALOW AT EPSOM, NEW ZEALAND          CHILWELL AND TREVITHICK, ARCHITECTS

HOUSE AT INVERCARGILL, NEW ZEALAND          EDMUND R. WILSON, ARCHITECT

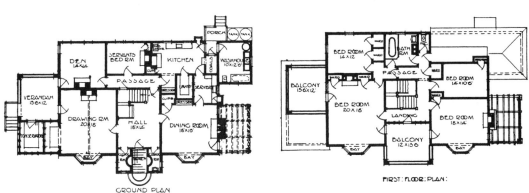

GROUND PLAN

FIRST · FLOOR · PLAN

HOUSE AT REMUERA, AUCKLAND
GERALD E. JONES, ARCHITECT

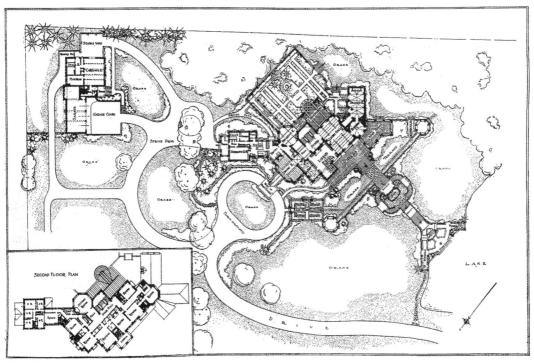

HOUSE AT ST. DAVIDS, PENNSYLVANIA
D. KNICKERBACKER BOYD, ARCHITECT

HOUSE AT ST. DAVIDS, PENNSYLVANIA
THE GARAGE AND GATE LODGE

D. KNICKERBACKER BOYD, ARCHITECT

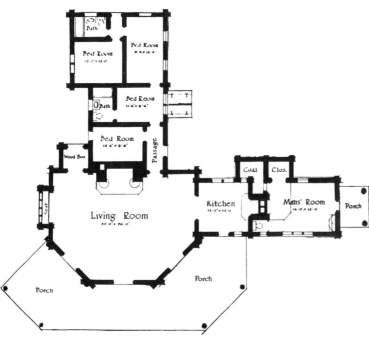

HOUSE AT ST. DAVIDS, PENNSYLVANIA—THE LOG
CABIN.  D. KNICKERBACKER BOYD, ARCHITECT

HOUSE AT WYNNEWOOD, PENNSYLVANIA  L. V. BOYD, ARCHITECT

"OAK KNOLL," PASADENA, CALIFORNIA                    ELMER GREY, ARCHITECT

GREATWOOD DWELLING, OTTER-
SHAW—THE HALL. M. H. BAILLIE
SCOTT, ARCHITECT

DESIGN FOR A BOUDOIR. BY H. DAVIS RICHTER, R.B.A.

SYDNEY R. JONES–OPEN FIREPLACE

WATER-GARDEN DESIGNED BY LAWRENCE GRANT WHITE ARCHITECT. BRONZE FOUNTAIN GROUP BY JANET SCUDDER

THE "PULITZER" RESIDENCE—THE SWIMMING POOL
DESIGNED BY CHARLES A. PLATT, ARCHITECT

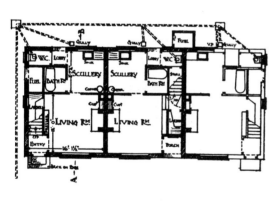

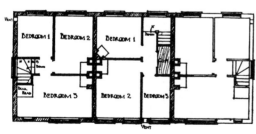

THREE COTTAGES AT WALGRAVE
GORDON ALLEN, F.R.I.B.A., ARCHITECT

"WALLINGFORD," PURLEY—THE GARDEN FRONT

SYDNEY TATCHELL, F.R.I.B.A., ARCHITECT

HALL FIREPLACE AT "THE WHITE HOUSE," GREAT CHART
DESIGNED BY M. H. BAILLIE SCOTT, ARCHITECT

HOUSES AT WAKE GREEN, NEAR BIRMINGHAM
COSSINS, PEACOCK AND BEWLAY, ARCHITECTS

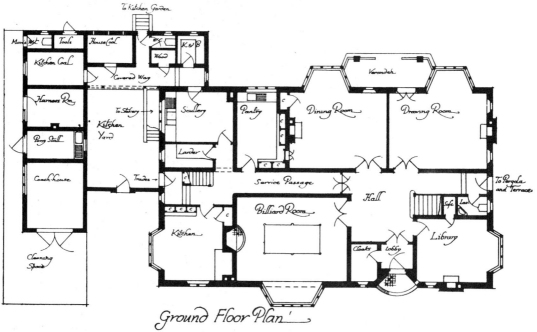

Ground Floor Plan

"WALLINGFORD," PURLEY. SYDNEY
TATCHELL, F.R.I.B.A., ARCHITECT

"WALLINGFORD," PURLEY—THE GARDEN FRONT
SYDNEY TATCHELL, F.R.I.B.A., ARCHITECT

THE "PRATT" RESIDENCE, GLEN COVE, L.I.
TROWBRIDGE AND ACKERMAN, ARCHITECTS

HOUSE AT FULMER, BUCKS.  UNSWORTH AND TRIGGS, ARCHITECTS

"ARDKINGLAS," CAIRNDOW (*Photo Thos. Lewis*)   SIR ROBERT LORIMER, A.R.S.A., F.R.I.B.A., ARCHITECT

"POLLARD'S WOOD GRANGE," BUCKS.—ENTRANCE LODGE   J: E. FORBES AND J. D. TATE, FF.R.I.B.A., ARCHITECTS

*Photo Thos. Lewis*

"NETHER CABERSTONE," WAL-
KERBURN.   JAMES B. DUNN,
A.R.S.A., F.R.I.B.A., ARCHITECT

M. H. BAILLIE SCOTT—A SMALL COUNTRY HOUSE—ENTRANCE FRONT

**SYDNEY R. JONES**
PAIR OF STONE COTTAGES. SUITABLE FOR
THE COTSWOLD COUNTRY

**SYDNEY R. JONES**
PAIR OF CONCRETE COTTAGES

SCHEME FOR THE DECORATION
OF A COTTAGE INTERIOR,
HALL THORPE, R.B.A.

SCHEMES FOR THE DECORATION OF
COTTAGE INTERIORS. BY HALL THORPE, R.B.A.

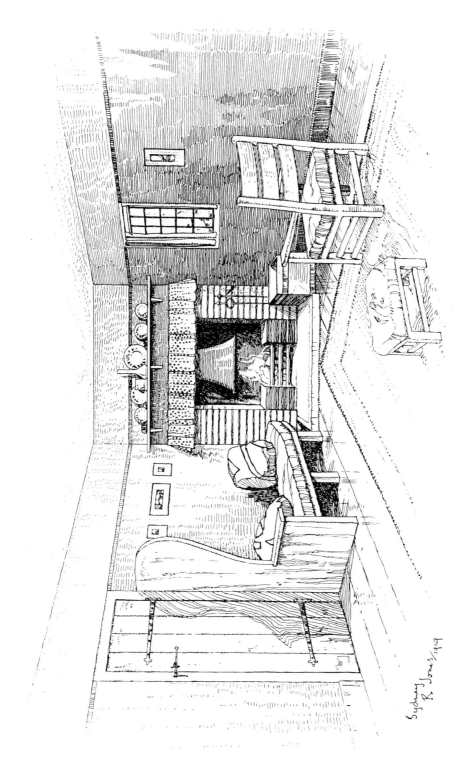

**SYDNEY R. JONES**
COTTAGE PARLOUR WITH CORNER FIREPLACE

Sydney
R. Jones 1919

SYDNEY R. JONES
LIVING-ROOM FOR SMALL COTTAGE

Sydney R Jones 1919

EASY CHAIR
UPHOLSTERED IN
TAPESTRY

DESIGNED BY
M. H. BAILLIE SCOTT
EXECUTED BY J. P. WHITE

DINING
CHAIR
IN MA-
HOGANY

DESIGNED BY
M. H. BAILLIE SCOTT
EXECUTED BY
J. P. WHITE

DINING
CHAIR
IN OAK

DESIGNED BY
M. H. BAILLIE SCOTT
EXECUTED BY
J. P. WHITE

GATE TABLE IN OAK

DESIGNED AND EXECUTED
BY HAMPTON & SONS, LTD.

ARMCHAIRS UPHOLSTERED IN
TAPESTRY.  DESIGNED AND
EXECUTED BY LIBERTY & CO., LTD.

BEDSTEAD IN MAHOGANY, INLAID
WITH PEWTER AND PINE-WOOD

BEDSTEAD IN OAK
WITH "KEYED" PANELS

BEDSTEAD IN OAK

BEDSTEAD IN OAK

DESIGNED BY AMBROSE HEAL, JUN.
EXECUTED BY HEAL & SON

BEDROOM SUITE IN CHESTNUT. DESIGNED BY AMBROSE HEAL, JUN. EXECUTED BY HEAL & SON

LOW SWING COT
WITH CURTAIN OF
EMBROIDERED LINEN

DESIGNED AND EXECUTED
BY LIBERTY & CO., LTD.

SWING COT WITH
CURTAIN OF
EMBROIDERED LINEN

DESIGNED AND EXECUTED BY
LIBERTY & CO., LTD.

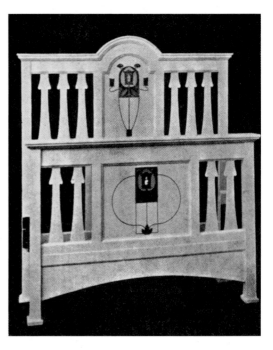

BEDSTEADS IN ENAMELLED WOOD INLAID WITH
COLOURED WOODS AND MOTHER-OF-PEARL

DESIGNED AND EXECUTED
BY SHAPLAND & PETTER, LTD.

FURNITURE PANELS DESIGNED AND CARVED
BY JOHN W. BENNETT, THE SCOTTISH GUILD OF HANDICRAFT, LTD.

SIDE TABLE IN OAK    DESIGNED AND EXECUTED BY
HAMPTON & SONS, LTD.

OCCASIONAL    DESIGNED BY
TABLE IN    M. H. BAILLIE SCOTT
MAHOGANY    EXECUTED BY
J. P. WHITE

TEA-TABLE IN    DESIGNED AND EXECUTED BY
MAHOGANY    LIBERTY & CO., LTD.

OCCASIONAL TABLE    DESIGNED AND EXECUTED BY
IN OAK    LIBERTY & CO., LTD.

CHAIRS IN OAK                    DESIGNED AND EXECUTED BY
                                ERNEST W. GIMSON

SETTEE IN OAK                         DESIGNED AND EXECUTED BY
                                      ERNEST W. GIMSON

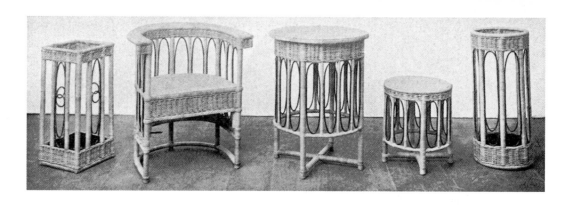

BASKET-WORK FURNITURE

DESIGNED BY W. SCHMIDT, EXECUTED BY THE
PRAG-RUDNIKER KORBWAREN-FABRICATION

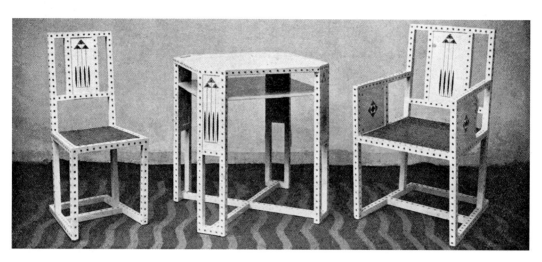

FURNITURE IN MAPLE
ENAMELLED WHITE

DESIGNED BY W. SCHMIDT, EXECUTED BY THE
PRAG-RUDNIKER KORBWAREN-FABRICATION

BENTWOOD FURNITURE

DESIGNED BY LEOPOLD BAUER, ARCHITECT
EXECUTED BY THONET BROS.

CABINET AND CHAIR AT CRESHAM HALL, N.B.
DESIGNED BY GEORGE WALTON, ARCHITECT

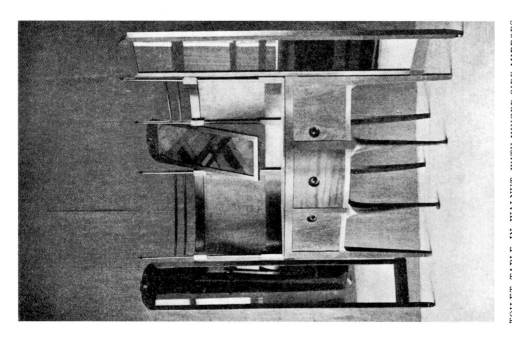

TOILET TABLE IN WALNUT WITH HINGED SIDE MIRRORS
DESIGNED BY GEORGE WALTON, ARCHITECT

FITTED OAK SIDEBOARD. DESIGNED
BY GEORGE WALTON, ARCHITECT

FURNITURE DESIGNED AND EXE-
CUTED BY MAURICE DUFRÊNE

BUREAU AND CHAIR          DESIGNED AND EXECUTED BY MAURICE DUFRÊNE

TABLE          DESIGNED AND EXECUTED BY TONY SELMERSHEIM

BOOKCASE        DESIGNED AND EXECUTED BY EUGÈNE GAILLARD

DINING-ROOM FURNITURE        DESIGNED AND EXECUTED BY MATHIEU GALLEREY

FURNITURE DESIGNED AND EXE-
CUTED BY LOUIS MAJORELLE

SIDEBOARD DESIGNED BY PROF. RICHARD RIEMERSCHMID,
EXECUTED BY THE DEUTSCHE WERKSTÄTTEN FÜR HAND-
WERKSKUNST, DRESDEN

BEDROOM FURNITURE IN MAHOGANY

DESIGNED BY MAX HEIDRICH
EXECUTED BY BERNARD STADLER

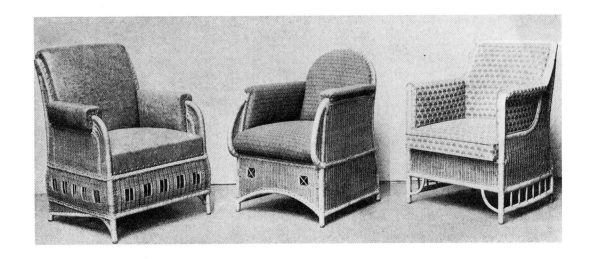

WICKER FURNITURE DESIGNED
BY M. A. NICOLAI, EXECUTED
BY DERICH AND SAUERTEIG

CHEST IN ENGLISH WALNUT INLAID    DESIGNED AND EXECUTED
WITH WALNUT AND CHERRY    BY ERNEST W. GIMSON

OCTAGONAL TABLE IN    DESIGNED AND EXECUTED
ENGLISH WALNUT    BY ERNEST W. GIMSON

INLAID SECRETAIRE CABINET IN ITALIAN
WALNUT DESIGNED BY W. A. S. BENSON,
EXECUTED BY MORRIS AND CO., LTD.

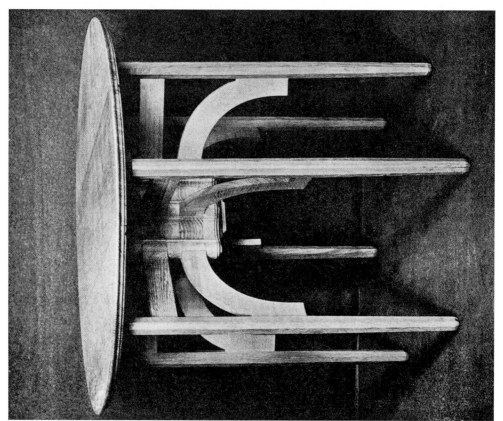

CHAIR AND TABLE IN OAK, DESIGNED BY C. F. A. VOYSEY, EXECUTED BY F. C. NIELSEN

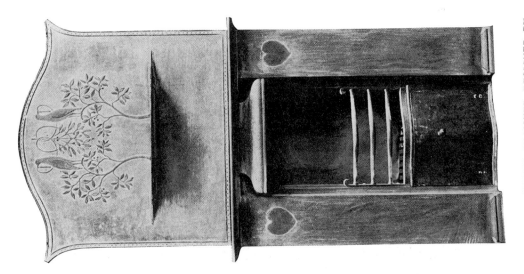

MANTEL REGISTER DESIGNED BY
C. F. A. VOYSEY, EXECUTED BY
LONGDEN AND CO.

MANTEL REGISTER DESIGNED BY C. F. A.
VOYSEY, EXECUTED BY GEO. WRIGHT, LTD.

CABINET IN MAHOGANY AND EBONY INLAID WITH
SILVER AND MOTHER-OF-PEARL, DESIGNED AND
EXECUTED BY ERNEST W. GIMSON

CABINET IN OAK    DESIGNED AND EXECUTED BY
SHAPLAND AND PETTER, LTD.

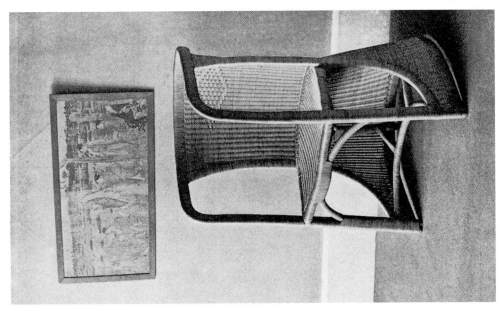

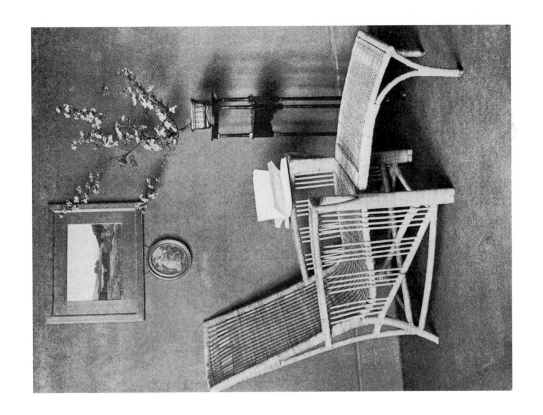

NURSERY FURNITURE AND DECORATION DESIGNED BY FANNY
HARLFINGER-ZAKUCKA.   FRIEZE BY PUPILS OF PROF. BÖHM

WICKER FURNITURE  DESIGNED BY M. A. NICOLAI, EXECUTED BY THEODOR REIMANN

NURSERY  DESIGNED BY PROF. ADELBERT NIEMEYER, EXECUTED BY THE
DEUTSCHE WERKSTÄTTEN FÜR HANDWERKSKUNST, MUNICH

CABINET DESIGNED BY PROF. OTTO PRUTSCHER, EXECUTED BY RICHARD LUDWIG

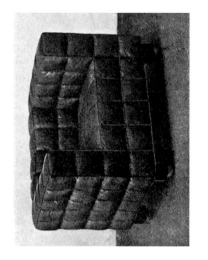

EASY-CHAIRS DESIGNED BY PROF. OTTO PRUTSCHER

CHEST DESIGNED BY PROF. OTTO PRUTSCHER, EXE-CUTED BY THE DEUTSCHE WERKSTAETTEN FÜR HANDWERKSKUNST, DRESDEN

WICKER FURNITURE DESIGNED BY JOSEF ZOTTI, EXECUTED BY THE PRAG-RUDNIKER KORBWARENFABRIK

WARDROBE IN ENGLISH WALNUT
DESIGNED AND EXECUTED BY ERNEST W. GIMSON

PAINTED CABINET IN WALNUT WITH BRASS FITTINGS, DESIGNED BY
RICHARD GARBE, WOODWORK BY G. GARBE, JUN., PAINTED DECORA-
TION BY RICHARD AND GERTRUDE GARBE

DESIGNED AND EXECUTED BY T. ROTHERHAM

DESIGNED BY HARRY H. PEACH

DESIGNED AND EXECUTED BY J. CRAMPTON

DRYAD FURNITURE

DESIGNED BY HANS DRÖSCHER AND WILHELM STEIN

DESIGNED BY M. A. NICOLAI

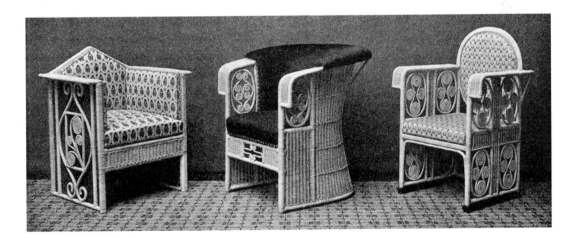

DESIGNED BY E. F. MARGOLD

WICKER ORNAMENTS AND CHAIRS EXE-
CUTED BY DERICHS AND SAUERTEIG

CARVED OAK SETTLE DESIGNED AND
EXECUTED BY JOHN W. BENNETT

DESIGNED BY H. H. PEACH

DESIGNED BY B. J. FLETCHER

"DRYAD" FURNITURE

WICKER CHAIRS DESIGNED BY JOSEF ZOTTI, EXECUTED BY THE PRAG RUDNIKER KORBWARENFABRIK
PRINTED LINEN DESIGNED BY ANTON HOFER

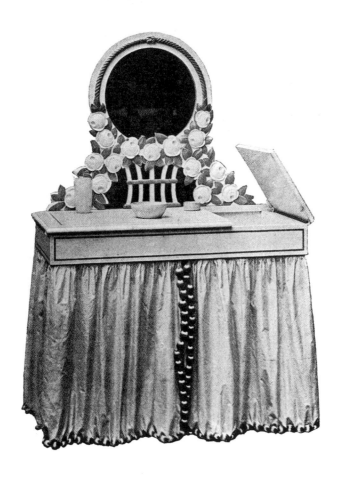

TOILET-TABLE AND SIDE-BOARD DESIGNED
AND EXECUTED BY ANDRE GROULT

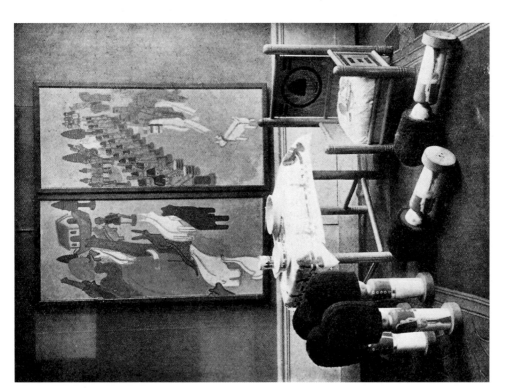

NURSERY FURNITURE AND TOYS DESIGNED BY ANDRÉ HELLÉ, EXECUTED BY THE MAGASINS DU PRINTEMPS

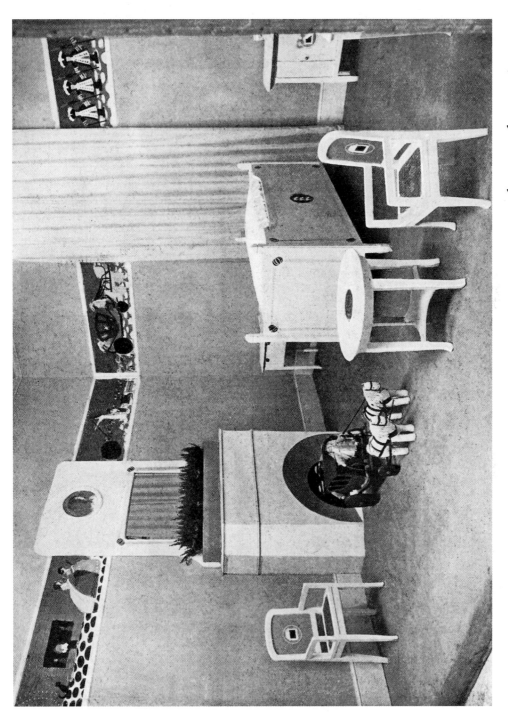

NURSERY DESIGNED BY ANDRÉ HELLÉ, EXECUTED BY THE MAGASINS DU PRINTEMPS; FRIEZE BY MADAME HELLÉ

MAHOGANY DRESSING-TABLE AND STOOL.   DESIGNED BY M. H. BAILLIE-SCOTT

*(Drawn by Allen Chandler)*

BEDROOM FURNITURE IN MAHOGANY.   DESIGNED BY M. H.
BAILLIE  SCOTT, EXECUTED BY STORY AND CO., KENSINGTON

DRESSING-TABLE DESIGNED
BY JESSIE BAYES

CHERRY-WOOD CABINET FOR PRINTS
WITH DOOR PANELS OF INCISED LACQUER
DESIGNED BY FRANK BRANGWYN, A.R.A.

DESIGN BY FRANK BRANGWYN,
A.R.A., FOR DOORS OF A
CABINET, EXECUTED IN
INCISED LACQUER

RUSH-SEATED CHAIR

HORN LANTERN

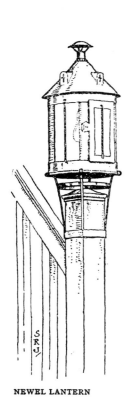

NEWEL LANTERN

COMBINED BOOK-SHELVES AND WRITING-DESK

FURNITURE BY SYDNEY R. JONES

DORMER WINDOW WITH FITTED DRESSING-TABLE AND CHEST

FITTED WARDROBE WITH SHELF, HANGING CUPBOARD, AND MOVABLE TRAYS

FURNITURE BY SYDNEY R. JONES

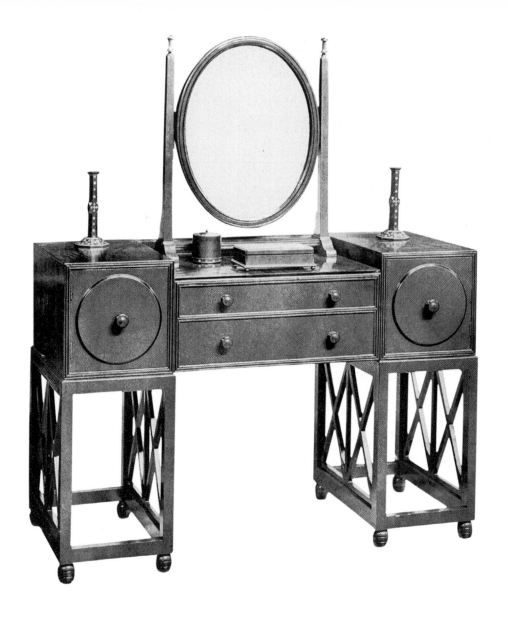

TOILET TABLE PAINTED EMERALD GREEN
WITH BLACK LINES. DESIGNED BY AMBROSE
HEAL, EXECUTED BY HEAL AND SON

PAINTED BOOKCASE.   DESIGNED BY
THE  LATE  LIEUT.  NOEL  SIMMONS

SMALL DRESSER
WITH SHELF FOR
BOOKS OR PLATES

CHAIR AND OR-
DINARY KITCHEN
TABLE WITH
DRAWER

FURNITURE DESIGNED
BY PERCY A. WELLS

WARDROBE
WITH "THREE-
PLY" PANELS

TOWEL - HORSE
AND CHEST OF
DRAWERS WITH
CUPBOARD

FURNITURE DESIGNED
BY PERCY A. WELLS

CHAIR WITH
BIRCH SEAT
AND DRESSING-
TABLE WITH
SWING GLASS

PAINTED CHEST
OF DRAWERS
WITH GLASS

FURNITURE DESIGNED
BY PERCY A. WELLS

DRESSER IN
WHITEWOOD
WITH SHELVES

DWARF DRESSER
WITHOUT TOP
SHELVES

FURNITURE DESIGNED
BY PERCY A. WELLS

SYDNEY R. JONES
COTTAGE FURNITURE DESIGNED AND
EXECUTED BY HEAL AND SON

Sydney R. Jones
1919

**SYDNEY R. JONES**
COTTAGE FURNITURE DESIGNED AND
EXECUTED BY HEAL AND SON

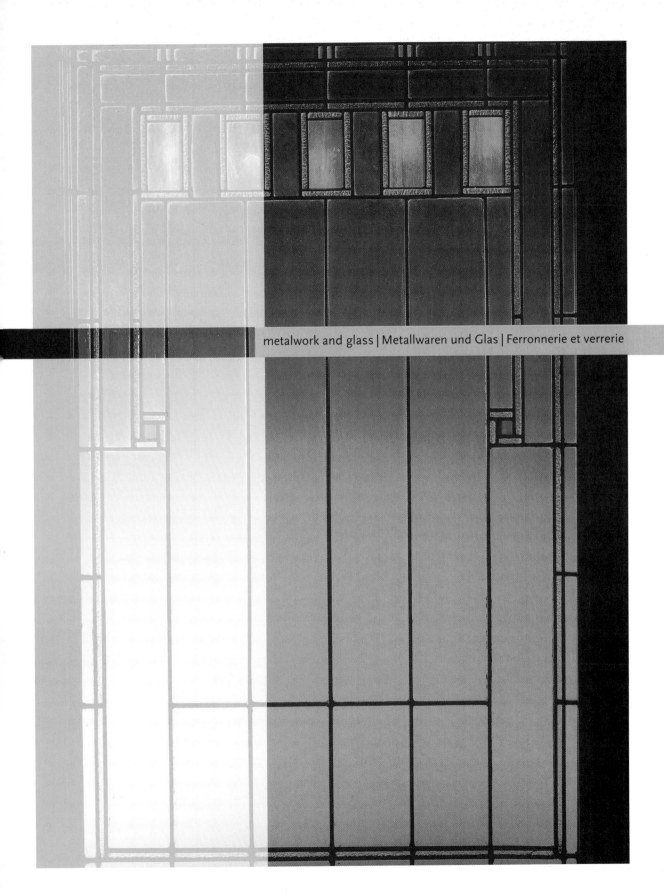

metalwork and glass | Metallwaren und Glas | Ferronnerie et verrerie

SILVER BOWL AND PLINTH
DESIGNED AND EXECUTED BY LIBERTY & CO., LTD.

S.LVER HOT-WATER JUG
DESIGNED AND EXECUTED BY G. L. CONNELL

SILVER AND COPPER CASKET,
SILVER TEA CADDY AND BOWL

DESIGNED AND EXECUTED BY A. E. JONES

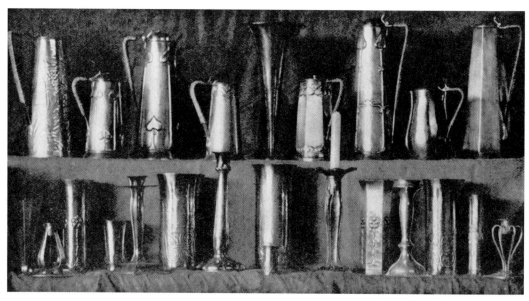

COPPER WARE

DESIGNED AND EXECUTED BY THE
KESWICK SCHOOL OF INDUSTRIAL ARTS

SILVER AND COPPER CASKET, SILVER
CANDLESTICK AND BOWL

DESIGNED AND EXECUTED BY A. E. JONES

SILVER AND ENAMEL DISH AND SPOON

DESIGNED AND EXECUTED BY W. S. HADAWAY

BEATEN SILVER FRUIT BOWL AND
FLOWER VASES

DESIGNED AND EXECUTED BY THE
GOLDSMITHS' AND SILVERSMITHS' CO., LTD.

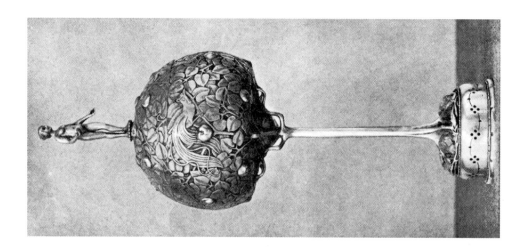

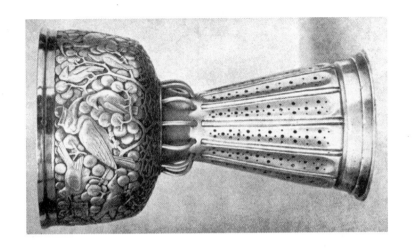

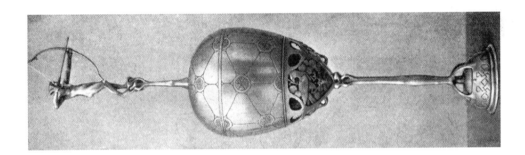

DESIGNED BY OTTO PRUTSCHER, ARCHITECT

DESIGNED BY E. HOPPE, ARCHITECT

DESIGNED BY E. HOPPE, ARCHITECT

TABLE GLASS EXECUTED BY BAKALOWITZ UND SÖHNE

TABLE GLASS DESIGNED AND EXECUTED
BY JAMES POWELL AND SONS

TABLE GLASS DESIGNED AND EXECUTED
BY JAMES POWELL AND SONS

SILVER DESSERT PLATES DESIGNED AND EXECUTED
BY W. S. HADAWAY AND F. LUTIGER

FRUIT-DISH IN SILVER WITH GILDING. DESIGNED AND
EXECUTED BY PROF. ERNST RIEGEL

COCOA-NUT CUP WITH SILVER MOUNTING AND GILDING.
DESIGNED AND EXECUTED BY PROF. ERNST RIEGEL

IRON WORK STUDDED WITH BRASS NAILS
DESIGNED BY PROF. ERNST RIEGEL

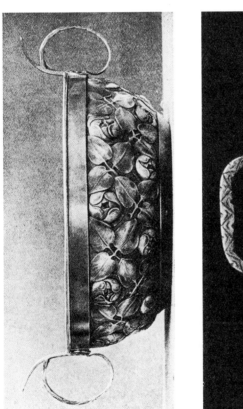

SILVER FRUIT-DISH AND STEEL CASKET DESIGNED AND
EXECUTED BY PROF. ERNST RIEGEL

TOAST RACK, JUG, CRUET AND TABLE
SILVER, DESIGNED BY C. F. A. VOYSEY

CLOCKS IN WROUGHT IRON DESIGNED BY LUDWIG HOHL-WEIN, EXECUTED BY JOSEF ZIMMERMANN AND CO.

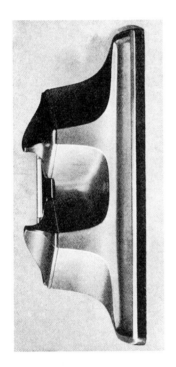

INKSTAND AND CLOCK IN CAST IRON. DESIGNED BY PROF. ALBIN MÜLLER, EXECUTED BY THE FÜRSTLICH STOLLBERG'SCHES HÜTTENAMT

GRANITE AND BRONZE CLOCK WITH IVORY AND MOTHER-OF-PEARL DECORATION, DESIGNED AND EXECUTED BY A. REIMANN

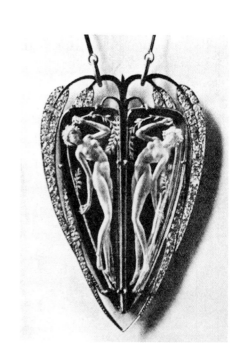

JEWELRY AND SILVERWORK DESIGNED
AND EXECUTED BY RENÉ LALIQUE

METAL-WORK DESIGNED AND
EXECUTED BY J. PAUL COOPER

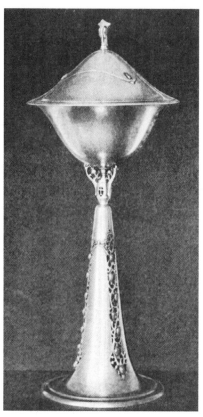

SILVER TEA AND COFFEE SERVICE DESIGNED
BY F. ADLER AND SILVER CUPS DESIGNED
BY PROF. PAUL HAUSTEIN, EXECUTED BY
P. BRUCKMANN UND SÖHNE

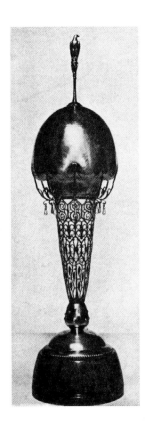

SILVER DISH DESIGNED BY BERNARD WENIG
SILVER CUPS DESIGNED BY CARL STOCK
EXECUTED BY PETER BRUCKMANN UND SÖHNE

SILVER FRUIT STANDS DESIGNED BY
HANS BOLAK, AND GOBLETS DESIGNED
BY GUSTAV KALHAMMER AND HAUSLER
EXECUTED BY EDWARD FRIEDMANN

JEWEL CASKET DESIGNED AND EXECUTED BY CARL POLLER

EBONY WORK-BOX WITH ENAMEL FILLINGS, AND COPPER JEWEL CASKET WITH ENAMEL LID, DESIGNED AND EXECUTED BY ADELE VON STARK

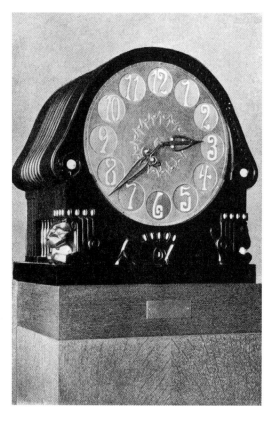

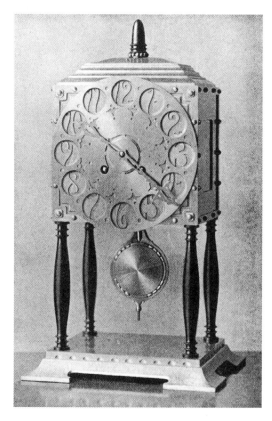

JEWEL CASKET IN EBONY AND MOTHER-OF-PEARL,
SET WITH OPALS. CLOCKS IN EBONY, IVORY AND
BRASS. DESIGNED BY ALFRED ALTHERR

COPPER BOWL WITH ENAMEL
FRIEZE SET WITH STONES
DESIGNED AND EXECUTED
BY EUGEN EHRENBÖCK

COPPER MIRROR WITH BLUE ENAMEL
DESIGNED AND EXECUTED BY EUGEN
EHRENBÖCK

DESIGNED BY PROF. JOSEF HOFFMANN

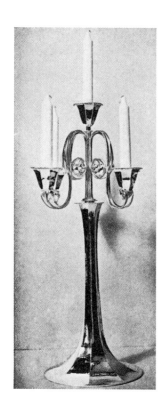

DESIGNED BY PROF. JOSEF
HOFFMANN

DESIGNED BY PROF. KOLO MOSER

DESIGNED BY PROF. JOSEF
HOFFMANN

FLOWER-STANDS AND SILVER CANDLESTICK
EXECUTED BY THE WIENER WERKSTAETTE

VASE AND CANDLESTICKS IN COPPER-GILT AND PIERCED BRASS. DESIGNED BY
EDWARD SPENCER, EXECUTED BY C. MOXEY, ERIC ROSS AND S. SMITH, OF
THE ARTIFICERS' GUILD

BRASS AND BRONZE SCONCES   DESIGNED BY EDWARD SPENCER, EXECUTED BY JOHN
BOWL AND STAND   GREEN AND ERIC ROSS, OF THE ARTIFICERS' GUILD

SILVER FRUIT BASKETS AND STAND DESIGNED
BY PROF. JOSEF HOFFMANN, EXECUTED BY
THE WIENER WERKSTAETTE, VIENNA

DESIGNED BY PROF.
JOSEF HOFFMANN

DESIGNED BY E. WIMMER

DESIGNED BY E. WIMMER

DESIGNED BY E. WIMMER

DESIGNED BY PROF. KOLO MOSER

DESIGNED BY PROF. JOSEF HOFFMANN

CRYSTAL AND SILVER FLOWER VASES, SILVER
CLOCK, SOUP-TUREEN AND CASKET, EXECUTED
BY THE WIENER WERKSTAETTE, VIENNA

CRYSTAL INK-STANDS
WITH ENAMEL LIDS

DESIGNED BY PROF. OTTO PRUTSCHER, EXE-
CUTED BY THE WIENER WERKSTAETTE

SILVER TEA AND COFFEE SERVICE
AND FRUIT STANDS

DESIGNED BY PROF. OTTO PRUTSCHER
EXECUTED BY E. FRIEDMANN

GLASS FRUIT-DISH, FLOWER-
VASES AND WINE-GLASSES

DESIGNED BY PROF. OTTO PRUTSCHER, EXE-
CUTED BY THE WIENER WERKSTAETTE

SILVER AND WALNUT FRUIT BOWLS
SILVER-PLATE SWEET-BOX AND DISH

DESIGNED BY EDWARD SPENCER, EXECUTED BY
C. MOXEY AND J. GREEN, OF THE ARTIFICERS' GUILD

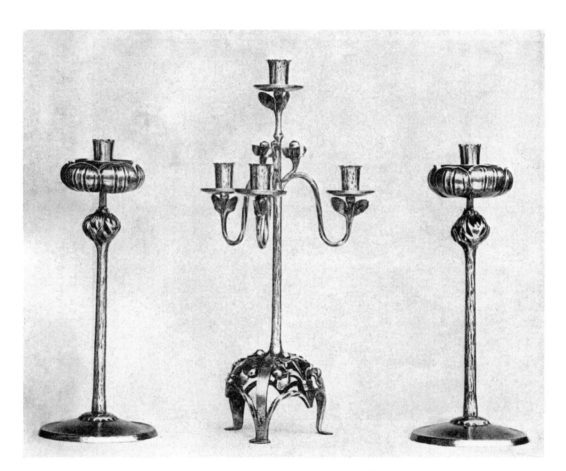

WROUGHT-IRON CANDLESTICKS

DESIGNED BY EDWARD SPENCER, EXECUTED BY
WALTER SPENCER, OF THE ARTIFICERS' GUILD

SILVER BOWL SET WITH CRYSTALS.   DESIGNED AND EXECUTED BY EDWARD
SPENCER, J. GREEN AND MEMBERS OF THE ARTIFICERS' GUILD

FRUIT STAND IN SILVER, IVORY AND ENAMEL, SET WITH PRECIOUS STONES
DESIGNED BY EDWARD SPENCER, EXECUTED BY ERIC ROSS, OF THE ARTIFI-
CERS' GUILD

EXECUTED BY E. FRIEDMANN

EXECUTED BY THE WIENER WERKSTAETTE

SILVER TEA AND COFFEE SERVICES
DESIGNED BY PROF. OTTO PRUTSCHER

EXECUTED BY OSKAR DIETRICH

EXECUTED BY FR. NAVRATIL

JEWEL-BOX AND FRUIT-DISH
DESIGNED BY HANS BOLEK

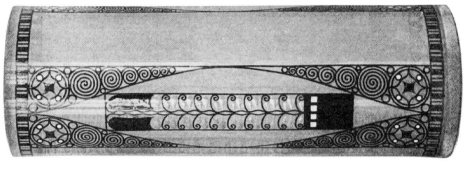

GLASS FLOWER-VASE

GLASS TRAY AND FRUIT-STAND

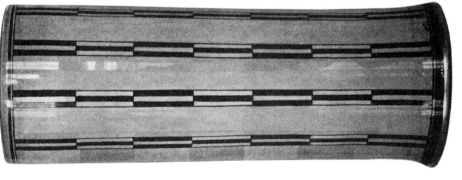

GLASS FLOWER-VASE

GLASSWARE DESIGNED AND EXECUTED IN THE IMPERIAL CRAFT SCHOOL AT STEINSCHÖNAU

GLASSWARE DESIGNED AND EXECUTED IN THE IMPERIAL CRAFT SCHOOL AT STEINSCHÖNAU

SILVER CUPS DESIGNED AND EXECUTED
BY PROF. ERNST RIEGEL

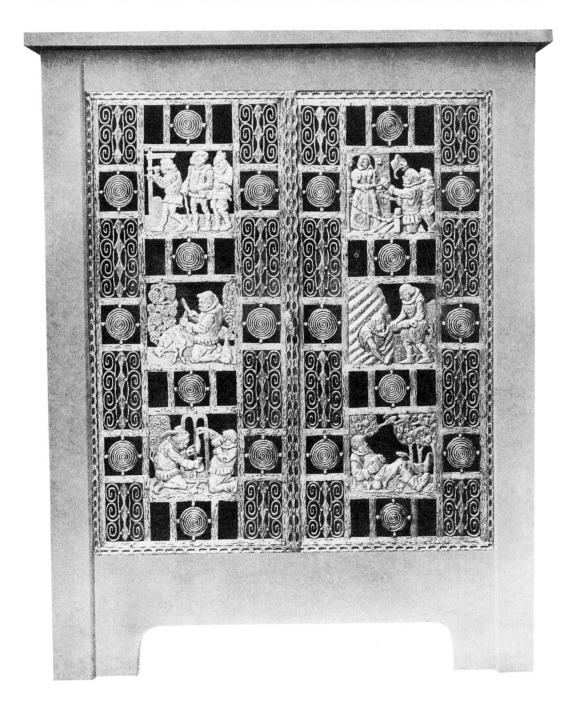

WROUGHT-IRON HEATING-MANTLE, WITH BRASS PANELS
DESIGNED AND EXECUTED BY REINHOLD KIRSCH

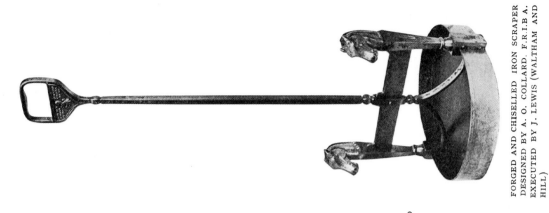

FORGED AND CHISELLED IRON SCRAPER
DESIGNED BY A. O. COLLARD. F.R.I.B.A.
EXECUTED BY J. LEWIS (WALTHAM AND
HILL)

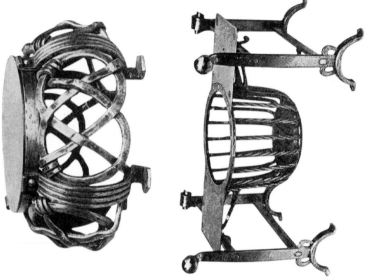

WROUGHT-IRON STAND AND GRATE. DESIGNED BY EDWARD
SPENCER, EXECUTED BY THE ARTIFICERS' GUILD

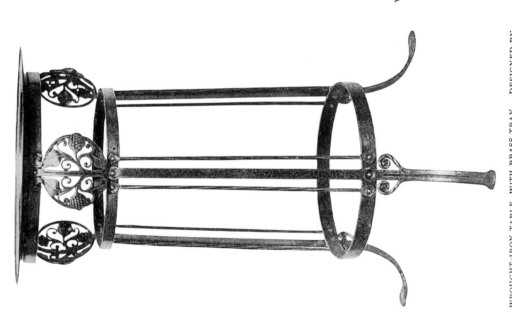

WROUGHT-IRON TABLE, WITH BRASS TRAY. DESIGNED BY
EDWARD SPENCER, EXECUTED BY THE ARTIFICERS' GUILD

SILVER CANDLESTICK. DESIGNED
BY EDWARD SPENCER, EXECUTED
BY THE ARTIFICERS' GUILD

TEA CADDY AND SPOON IN COPPER AND SILVER
DESIGNED BY EDWARD SPENCER, EXECUTED BY
THE ARTIFICERS' GUILD

SILVER TEAPOT. DESIGNED AND
EXECUTED BY HAROLD STABLER

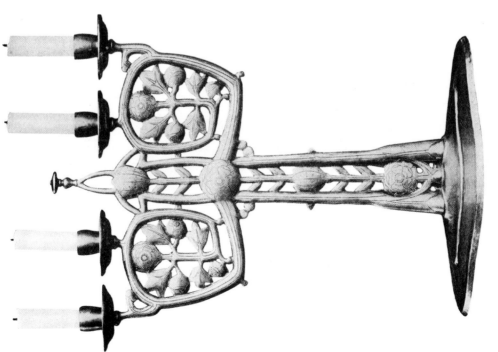

CANDLESTICK IN ENGRAVED BRASS. DESIGNED BY EDWARD SPENCER
EXECUTED BY THE ARTIFICERS' GUILD

DESIGNED BY KARL BERTSCH

DESIGNED BY KARL BERTSCH

DESIGNED BY ELSE REHM-VIETER

DESIGNED BY KARL BERTSCH

CLOCKS EXECUTED BY THE DEUTSCHE WERKSTÄTTEN
FÜR HANDWERKSKUNST, MUNICH

SILVER TEA SERVICE WITH IVORY HANDLES

DESIGNED BY EMANUEL JOSEF MARGOLD
EXECUTED BY P. BRUCKMANN UND SÖHNE

SILVER TEA SERVICE

DESIGNED BY FRANZ BÖRES, EXECUTED
BY P. BRUCKMANN UND SÖHNE

SILVER TEA SERVICE

DESIGNED BY FRITZ SCHMOLL VON EISENWERTH
EXECUTED BY P. BRUCKMANN UND SÖHNE

WROUGHT-IRON CANDLESTICKS DESIGNED BY EDWARD SPENCER, EXECUTED BY
WALTER SPENCER, OF THE ARTIFICERS' GUILD

STEEL SCONCES AND CANDLESTICKS DESIGNED BY EDWARD SPENCER, EXECUTED BY
FRANK GREEN AND FRANK JOBE, OF THE ARTIFICERS' GUILD

SILVER AND COPPER SALT-CELLARS,
SWEET - DISHES AND SUGAR-BASIN
DESIGNED BY EDWARD SPENCER
EXECUTED BY THE ARTIFICERS'
GUILD

BRASS LAMP DESIGNED AND
EXECUTED BY H. H. STANSFIELD
(CROMER GUILD OF HANDICRAFT)

COPPER HOT-WATER CAN DESIGNED
BY W. H. PICK, EXECUTED
BY THE DRYAD CRAFTSMEN

BRONZE AND WROUGHT-IRON FIRE-DOGS.   DESIGNED BY A. HAROLD SMITH, EXECUTED BY THE CARRON COMPANY

WROUGHT-IRON GATE FOR A GARDEN ENTRANCE
DESIGNED BY C. A. LLEWELYN ROBERTS
EXECUTED BY THE BIRMINGHAM GUILD

SILVER CARD-TRAY.   DESIGNED AND EXECUTED
BY H. R. FOWLER

SILVER ALMS DISH.   DESIGNED BY EDWARD SPENCER
EXECUTED BY THE ARTIFICERS' GUILD

BOWL IN SILVER AND ENAMEL

BOWL IN SILVER ON GILT STAND, SET WITH TURQUOISE, AMETHYSTS AND BLUE LAPIS

## METALWORK DESIGNED BY EDWARD SPENCER
## EXECUTED BY THE ARTIFICERS' GUILD

WROUGHT-IRON
GRATE WITH DOGS
DESIGNED BY
EDWARD SPENCER
EXECUTED BY
THE ARTIFICERS'
GUILD

WROUGHT-IRON AND BRASS GRATE AND DOGS.   EXECUTED BY THE ARTIFICERS' GUILD

GRATE, DOGS, AND FENDER        DESIGNED BY EDWARD SPENCER, EXECUTED BY THE ARTIFICERS' GUILD

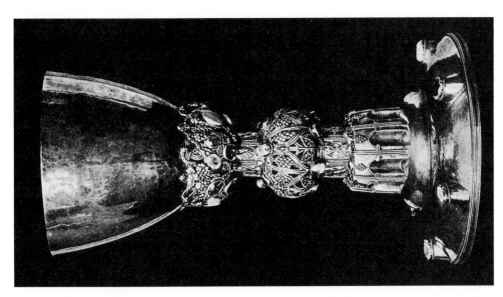

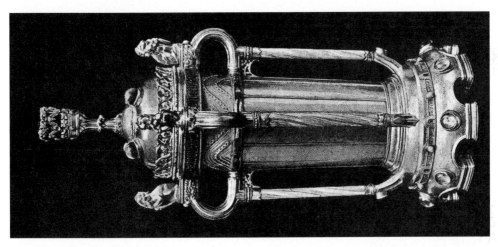

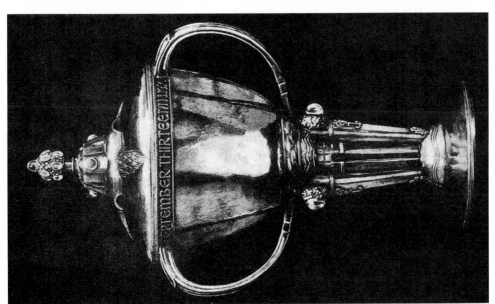

CUPS AND CHALICE IN SILVER, WITH GOLD ENRICHMENTS, ENAMEL, AND PRECIOUS STONES. DESIGNED BY EDWARD SPENCER, EXECUTED BY THE ARTIFICERS' GUILD

ceramics | Keramik | Céramiques

DESIGNED BY A. E. PEARCE

DESIGNED BY A. E. PEARCE

DESIGNED BY J. H. MOTT

DESIGNED BY A. E. PEARCE

GARDEN POTS IN TERRA-COTTA
EXECUTED BY DOULTON & CO., LTD., LAMBETH

GARDEN POT    DESIGNED BY MRS. G. F. WATTS
EXECUTED BY THE POTTERS' ARTS GUILD

GARDEN POT IN TERRA-COTTA
DESIGNED BY F. C. POPE
EXECUTED BY DOULTON & CO., LTD., LAMBETH

GARDEN POT IN TERRA-COTTA
DESIGNED BY F. C. POPE
EXECUTED BY DOULTON & CO., LTD., LAMBETH

GARDEN POT
DESIGNED BY MRS. G. F. WATTS
EXECUTED BY THE POTTERS' ARTS GUILD

TOILET WARE DESIGNED BY LÉON V. SOLON AND J. W. WADSWORTH
EXECUTED BY MINTONS LTD., FOR WARING & GILLOW, LTD., MANCHESTER.

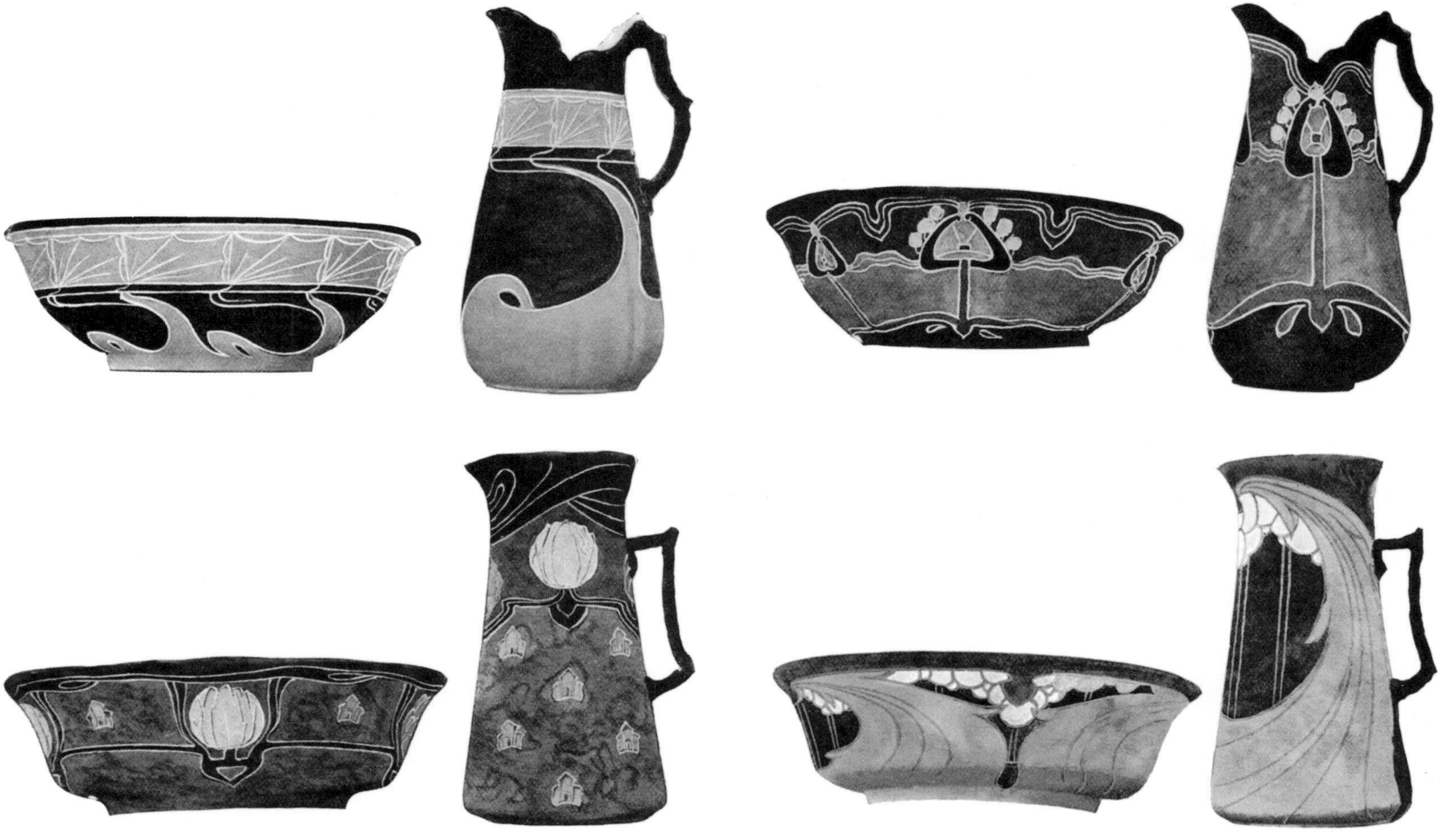

TOILET WARE DESIGNED AND
EXECUTED BY MINTONS, LTD.

DESIGNED BY JULTA SIKA

DESIGNED BY THERESA TRETHAN

DESIGNED BY THERESA TRETHAN

COFFEE AND DINNER SERVICES. EXECUTED
BY THE WIENER PORZELLAN–MANUFACTUR,
JOS. BÖCK

DESIGNED BY J. RAMB AND J. DORN

DESIGNED BY H. WIMMER AND THERESA TRETHAN

DESIGNED BY H. WIMMER AND KARL WITZMANN

TEA AND COFFEE SERVICES. EXECUTED BY
ERNST WAHLISS

DESIGN FOR NURSERY TILES BY JESSIE M. KING.

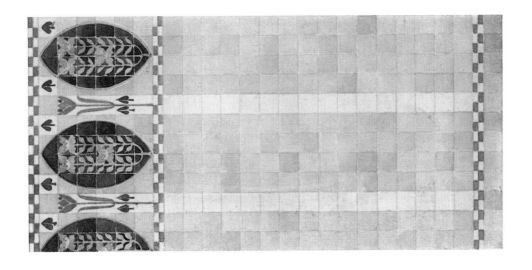

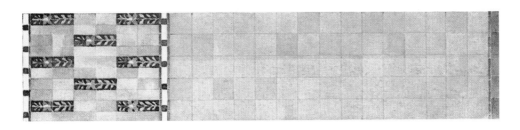

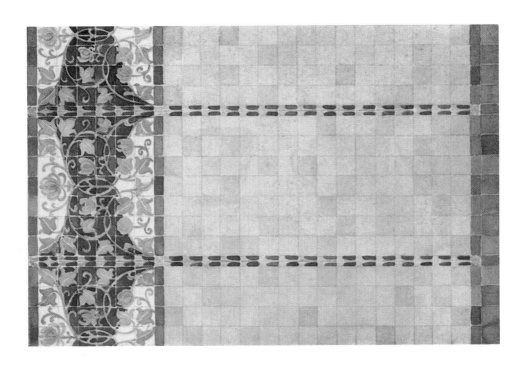

FAIENCE TILE WALL DECORATION DESIGNED BY A. E. PEARCE.
EXECUTED BY DOULTON & CO., LTD., LAMBETH.

GROUP OF RUSKIN POTTERY BY
W. HOWSON TAYLOR

GROUP OF POTTERY BY
ALFRED H. POWELL

PLAQUE. DESIGNED BY WALTER CRANE, R.W.S., AND PAINTED
BY RICHARD JOYCE FOR PILKINGTON'S TILE & POTTERY CO., LTD.

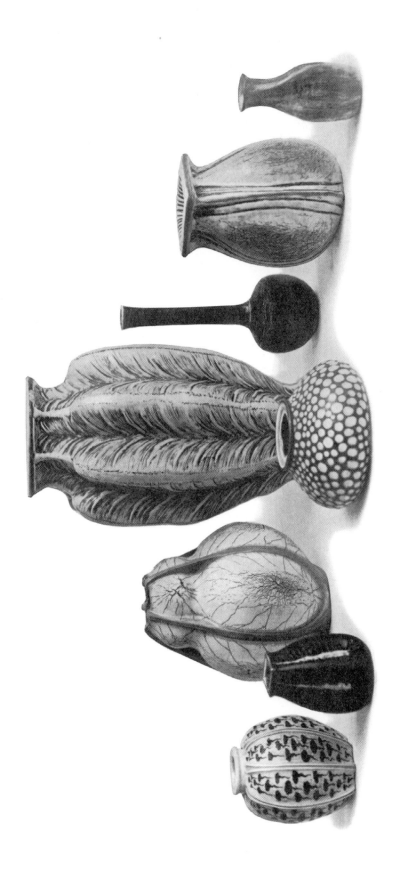

POTTERY

DESIGNED BY ELISABETH SCHMIDT-PECHT, EXECUTED BY F. A. PECHT

POTTERY DESIGNED BY PROFESSOR MAX LÄUGER
EXECUTED BY THE THONWERKE KANDERN (BADEN)

GROUP OF POTTERY      DESIGNED BY PROF. MAX LÄUGER, EXECUTED BY THE THONWERKE KANDERN

THURINGIAN POTTERY      EXECUTED AT THE DEUTSCHE-WERKSTÄTTEN FÜR HANDWERKSKUNST, DRESDEN

TEA SERVICE      DESIGNED BY PROF. ADELBERT NIEMEYER, EXECUTED BY THE ROYAL PORCELAIN MANUFACTORY, NYMPHENBURG

LUSTRE PLAQUES DESIGNED AND PAINTED
BY GORDON M. FORSYTH FOR PILKING-
TON'S TILE AND POTTERY CO., LTD.

DESIGN FOR A PAINTED BOWL BY CECIL JONES

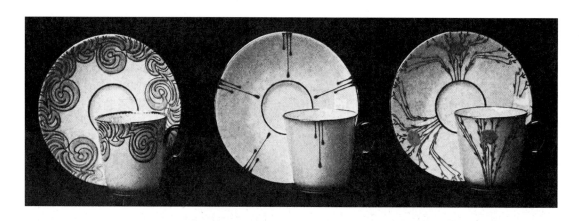

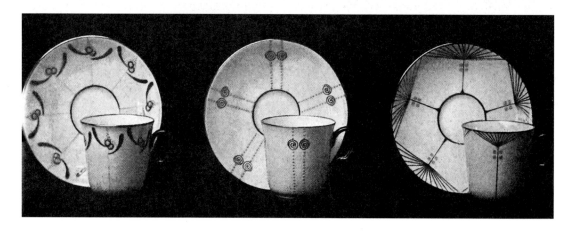

COFFEE SERVICES WITH ENAMEL
AND GOLD DECORATIONS, DE-
SIGNED BY JOHN W. WADSWORTH
EXECUTED BY MINTONS, LTD.

GROUP OF POTTERY DESIGNED
AND EXECUTED BY THE
MARTIN BROTHERS

GROUP OF "RUSKIN" POTTERY
DESIGNED AND EXECUTED BY
W. HOWSON TAYLOR

POTTERY DESIGNED BY ELISABETH SCHMIDT-
PECHT, EXECUTED BY J. A. PECHT

POTTERY DESIGNED BY ELISABETH SCHMIDT-
PECHT, EXECUTED BY J. A. PECHT

STONEWARE AND EARTHENWARE POTTERY
DESIGNED BY CHR. NEUREUTHER, EXECUTED
BY THE WAECHTERSBACHER STEINGUTFABRIK

POTTERY DESIGNED BY PROF. ALBIN MÜLLER AND PAUL
WYNAND, EXECUTED BY REINHOLD MERKELBACH

DESIGNED AND PAINTED
BY RICHARD JOYCE

DESIGNED AND PAINTED
BY W. S. MYCOCK

DESIGNED AND PAINTED
BY C. E. CUNDALL

DESIGNED AND PAINTED
BY RICHARD JOYCE

PILKINGTON'S "LANCASTRIAN LUSTRE" POTTERY

THE "BAGDAD" TAZZA, DESIGNED AND PAINTED BY GORDON M. FORSYTH.

THE "DAMASCUS" DISH.  DESIGNED AND PAINTED BY W. S. MYCOCK.

PILKINGTON'S "LANCASTRIAN LUSTRE" POTTERY.

"SERAPIS" POTTERY DESIGNED BY KARL
KLAUS, EXECUTED BY ERNST WAHLISS

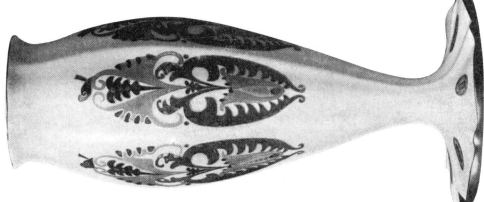

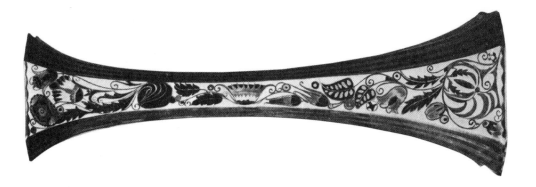

"SERAPIS" POTTERY DESIGNED BY KARL KLAUS, EXECUTED BY ERNST WAHLISS

UNDERGLAZE POTTERY. DISH BY ANNIE
P. MᴀᴄNICOL, JARS BY ANN MACBETH.

MAJOLICA PLATES DESIGNED BY PROF.
RIPPL-RÓNAI, EXECUTED BY THE ZSOLNAY
MANUFACTORY, PÉCS

MIRROR WITH PANELS OF LACQUERED WOOD
DESIGNED BY PROF. BERTHOLD LÖFFLER
EXECUTED BY THE WIENER WERKSTAETTE

CERAMIC FLOWER-VASES DESIGNED BY PROF.
MICHAEL POWOLNY, EXECUTED BY THE
WIENER KERAMIK-WERKSTAETTE

STONE FLOWER-VASE DESIGNED BY
J. ZOTTI, EXECUTED BY JUNG & RUSS

CERAMIC FRUIT-DISHES DESIGNED
AND EXECUTED BY HUGO F. KIRSCH

"RUSKIN" POTTERY.  DESIGNED AND
EXECUTED BY W. HOWSON TAYLOR

BOWL DESIGNED AND EXECUTED BY ANNIE P. MACNICOL

DISHES DESIGNED AND EXECUTED BY ALFRED H. AND LOUISE POWELL, FOR JOSIAH WEDGWOOD AND SONS

POTTERY DESIGNED AND EXECUTED BY THE ASHBY POTTERS' GUILD

PORCELAIN VASE DESIGNED BY PROF. ADELBERT NIEMEYER, EXECUTED
BY THE ROYAL PORCELAIN MANUFACTORY, NYMPHENBURG

PORCELAIN VASES AND COVERED JAR        DESIGNED BY PROF. ADELBERT NIEMEYER
EXECUTED BY GEBR. HEUBACH, LICHTE

PORCELAIN VASE DESIGNED AND EXECUTED
BY LÁSZLO VON MATTYASOVSZKY-ZSOLNAY

GROUP OF POTTERY DESIGNED AND EXECUTED
BY PROF. GIRA-JAKÓ

DESIGNED AND PAINTED BY GORDON M. FORSYTH

DESIGNED AND PAINTED BY GWLADYS M. RODGERS

# PILKINGTON'S "LANCASTRIAN LUSTRE" POTTERY

DESIGNED AND PAINTED BY W. S. MYCOCK

DESIGNED AND PAINTED BY ANNIE BURTON

# PILKINGTON'S "LANCASTRIAN LUSTRE" POTTERY

SMOKER'S SET EXECUTED BY REINHOLD MERKELBACH

COFFEE SERVICE EXECUTED BY MARZI UND REMY

STONEWARE DESIGNED
BY PROF. ALBIN MÜLLER

COFFEE SERVICE EXECUTED BY REINHOLD HANKE

TEA SERVICE EXECUTED BY S. P GERZ

STONEWARE  DESIGNED
BY PROF. ALBIN MÜLLER

EXECUTED BY J. W. REMY     EXECUTED BY J. P. THEWALD     EXECUTED BY DÜMLER UND BREIDEN

## STONEWARE JUGS DESIGNED
## BY PROF. ALBIN MÜLLER

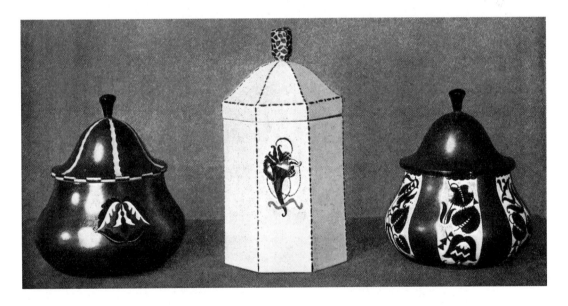

CERAMIC FRUIT DISH AND COVERED JARS
DESIGNED BY DAGOBERT PECHE, EXECUTED BY
THE VEREINIGTE WIENER UND GMUNDENER
KERAMIKFABRIK SCHLEISS GESELLSCHATF

EARTHENWARE DISH DESIGNED
BY CHAS. E. E. CONNOR, EXECUTED
BY JOSIAH WEDGWOOD AND SONS

PAPER-WEIGHT

CHILD'S BREAD-AND-MILK SET

MILK PITCHER

POTTERY DESIGNED BY EDITH
BROWN, EXECUTED BY THE
PAUL REVERE POTTERY

PANEL DESIGNED BY JOHN DEE WAREHAM, EXECUTED BY THE ROOKWOOD POTTERY

LIVING-ROOM MANTEL DESIGNED BY JOHN DEE WAREHAM, EXECUTED BY THE ROOKWOOD POTTERY

OVERMANTEL DESIGNED BY JOHN DEE WAREHAM, EXECUTED BY THE ROOKWOOD POTTERY

" TOTEM POLE " MANTEL DESIGNED BY MARX AND JONES, EXECUTED BY THE ROOKWOOD POTTERY

DISHES DECORATED IN UNDERGLAZE
COLOURS BY CHARLES E. E. CONNOR
AT JOSIAH WEDGWOOD AND SONS' POTTERY

GROUP OF "RUSKIN" POTTERY DESIGNED
AND EXECUTED BY W. HOWSON TAYLOR

GROUP OF POTTERY DESIGNED AND PAINTED BY ALFRED H. AND LOUISE POWELL

LARGE LUSTRE VASE DESIGNED AND PAINTED BY LOUISE POWEL

POTTERY DESIGNED AND PAINTED
BY ALFRED H. AND LOUISE POWELL

MURAL PANELS

DESIGNED BY LAUB AND HELVING, EXECUTED
BY THE ROOKWOOD POTTERY

GROUP OF SOFT PORCELAIN

DESIGNED AND EXECUTED BY THE ROOKWOOD POTTERY

EXTERIOR PANEL DESIGNED AND EXECUTED
BY THE ROOKWOOD POTTERY

BOWL DESIGNED AND EXECUTED BY
DOROTHEA WARREN·O'HARA

TABLE-WARE

DESIGNED AND EXECUTED BY DOROTHEA WARREN·O'HARA

DESIGNED BY G. M. RODGERS

DESIGNED BY G. M. FORSYTH

DESIGNED BY W. S. MYCOCK

DESIGNED BY W. S. MYCOCK

POTTERY DESIGNED AND PAINTED
BY GABRIEL C. BUNNEY, EXECUTED
BY JOSIAH WEDGWOOD AND SONS

SILVER AND RUBY LUSTRE
DESIGNED AND PAINTED BY GORDON M. FORSYTH

SILVER AND PERSIAN LUSTRES
DESIGNED AND PAINTED BY W. S. MYCOCK

SILVER AND RUBY LUSTRE
DESIGNED AND PAINTED BY RICHARD JOYCE

SILVER AND PERSIAN LUSTRES
DESIGNED AND PAINTED BY RICHARD JOYCE

PILKINGTON'S "LANCASTRIAN LUSTRE" POTTERY

SILVER AND RUBY LUSTRE ON IVORY GROUND    PAINTED BY C. E. CUNDALL

SILVER AND PERSIAN LUSTRES
DESIGNED AND PAINTED BY RICHARD JOYCE

SILVER AND RUBY LUSTRE
DESIGNED AND PAINTED BY GORDON M. FORSYTH

## PILKINGTON'S "LANCASTRIAN LUSTRE" POTTERY

POTTERY DESIGNED AND PAINTED
BY ALFRED H. AND LOUISE POWELL

POTTERY DESIGNED AND PAINTED
BY ALFRED H. AND LOUISE POWELL

DESIGNED AND PAINTED
BY RICHARD JOYCE

DESIGNED AND PAINTED
BY W. S. MYCOCK

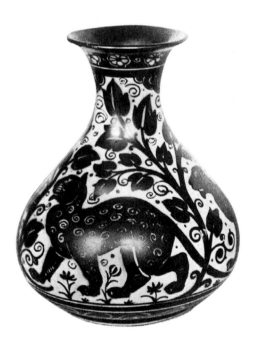

DESIGNED AND PAINTED
BY RICHARD JOYCE

DESIGNED AND PAINTED
BY RICHARD JOYCE

# PILKINGTON'S "LANCASTRIAN LUSTRE" POTTERY

COFFEE SET MADE FOR HEAL AND SON BY COPELAND AND CO.

KITCHEN SET MADE FOR HEAL AND SON BY J. WEDGWOOD AND SONS

POTTERY DESIGNED AND PAINTED BY
DORA LUNN (THE RAVENSCOURT POTTERY)

POTTERY DESIGNED AND
PAINTED BY DORA LUNN
(THE RAVENSCOURT POTTERY)

POTTERY DESIGNED AND
PAINTED BY DORA LUNN
(THE RAVENSCOURT POTTERY)

*Fr    drawings by Dora Stone*

POTTERY DESIGNED AND
PAINTED BY DORA LUNN
(THE RAVENSCOURT POTTERY)

GREY PORCELAIN PLAQUE
DESIGNED BY OLAF JENSEN
EXECUTED BY THE ROYAL CO-
PENHAGEN PORCELAIN COMPANY

GREY PORCELAIN PLAQUE
DESIGNED BY OLAF JENSEN
EXECUTED BY THE ROYAL CO-
PENHAGEN PORCELAIN COMPANY

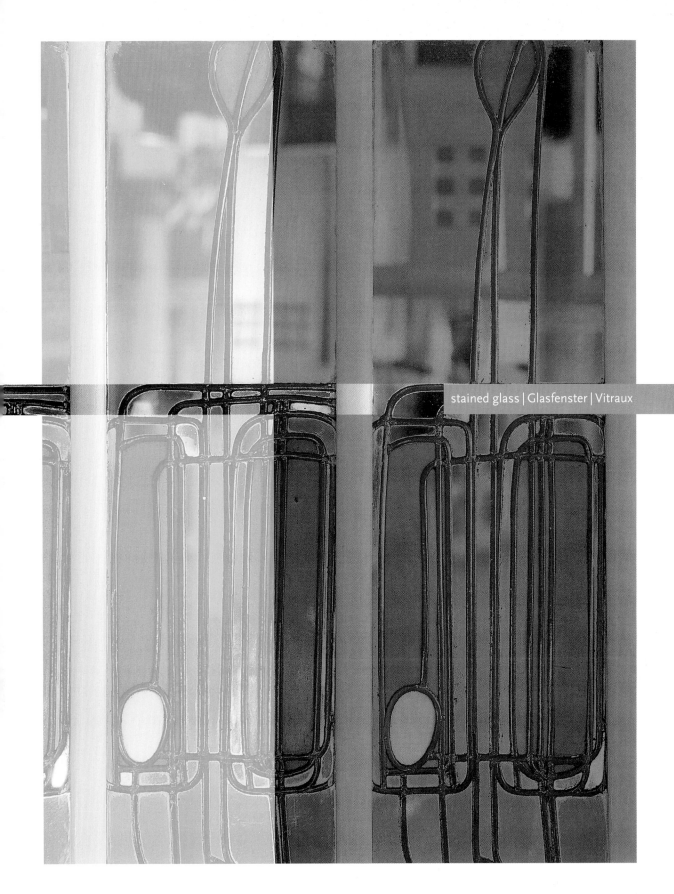

stained glass | Glasfenster | Vitraux

WINDOW DESIGNED AND EXECUTED BY OSCAR PATERSON.

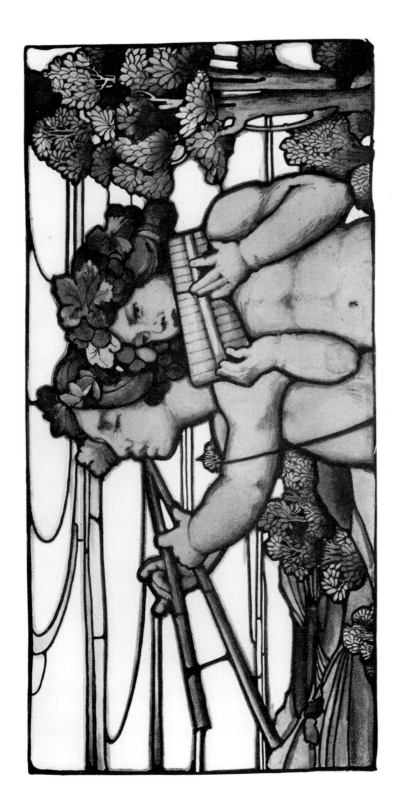

WINDOW DESIGNED AND EXECUTED BY J. S. MELVILLE FOR OSCAR PATERSON.

WINDOW DESIGNED BY ALEX. GASCOYNE.
EXECUTED BY GEO. F. GASCOYNE & SON.

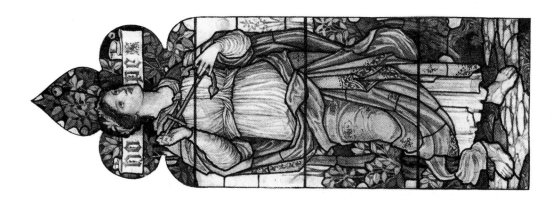

MIRROR BY RAYMOND SUBES, 131, RUE DAMIEMONT, PARIS

WROUGHT IRON GRILL BY PAUL KISS, PARIS

HALL WINDOW DESIGNED BY E. A. TAYLOR.
EXECUTED BY GEORGE WRAGGE, LTD.

WINDOW "THE AMBUSH." DESIGNED
AND EXECUTED BY OSCAR PATERSON.

1907 · stained glass · **447**

WINDOW. "THE YOUTH OF BACCHUS." DESIGNED AND EXECUTED BY WM. MORRIS & CO., WESTMINSTER.

HALL AND LANDING WINDOWS.  DESIGNED BY
ALEX. GASCOYNE.  EXECUTED BY GEO. F. GASCOYNE & SON.

WINDOW DESIGNED BY OSCAR PATERSON
EXECUTED BY PETER GRANT AND JAMES LEAT.

STAIRCASE WINDOW DE-
SIGNED BY ALEXANDER GASCOYNE.

1909 · stained glass · **451**

DRAWING-ROOM WINDOW DESIGNED BY
E. A. TAYLOR, EXECUTED BY GEO. WRAGGE, LTD.

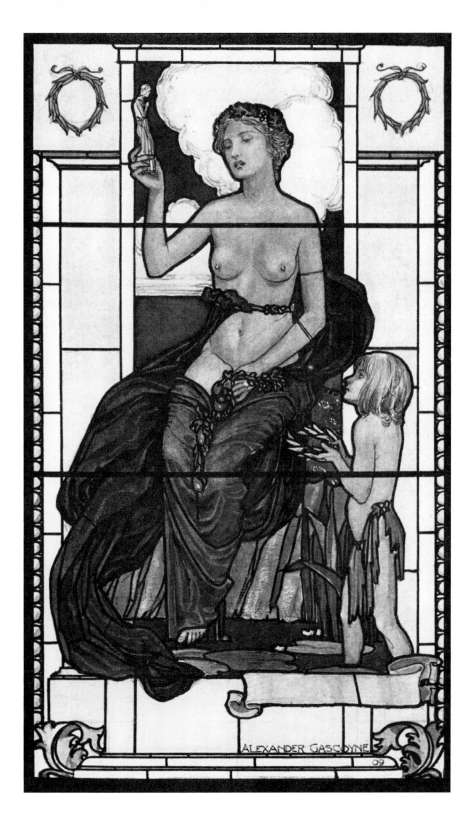

HALL WINDOW DESIGNED BY ALEXANDER GASCOYNE
EXECUTED BY GEO. F. GASCOYNE AND SON.

WINDOWS DESIGNED BY ARTHUR A. ORR
EXECUTED BY ARTHUR J. DIX.

DESIGNED BY JAMES H. LEAT.

DESIGNED BY JAMES HILL.

DESIGNED BY JAMES H. LEAT.

WINDOW DESIGNED BY PROF. KOLO MOSER
EXECUTED BY CARL GEYLING'S ERBEN

DESIGN FOR A WINDOW BY J. EDGAR MITCHELL
EXECUTED IN ANTIQUE GLASS

WINDOWS DESIGNED BY M. V. BREITMAYER.

STAINED GLASS WINDOWS DESIGNED AND
EXECUTED IN THE TIFFANY STUDIOS

WINDOW DESIGNED BY E. A. TAYLOR
EXECUTED BY GEORGE RHIND

ROSE LEAVES

FOR THE WORLD

WINDOW DESIGNED BY E. A. TAYLOR
EXECUTED BY GEORGE RHIND

WINDOW FOR DRAWING-ROOM
INGLE.  DESIGNED AND EXECUTED
BY E. A. TAYLOR

KIRKCVDBRIGHT

LANDING WINDOW.  DESIGNED AND
EXECUTED BY E. A. TAYLOR

GLASS MOSAIC PANELS. DESIGNED AND
EXECUTED BY ANDREW STODDART

WINDOWS DESIGNED BY JOHN C. HALL
EXECUTED BY JOHN C. HALL AND CO.

lighting | Lampen | Luminaires

CANDLESTICKS    DESIGNED BY H. STAHLER
EXECUTED BY JESSON, BIRKETT & CO., LTD.

TABLE LAMP IN    DESIGNED AND EXECUTED
HAMMERED IRON    BY THE GUILD OF
AND COPPER    HANDICRAFT, LTD.

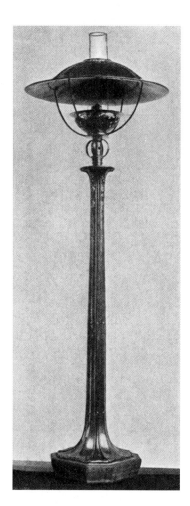

NEWEL-POST LAMP IN
WROUGHT COPPER
    DESIGNED BY C. A. LL. ROBERTS
    EXECUTED BY E. & R. GITTINS

TABLE LAMPS    DESIGNED BY E. SPENCER
EXECUTED BY THE ARTIFICERS' GUILD, LTD.

STANDARD LAMP IN BRASS
DESIGNED AND EXECUTED
BY N. & E. SPITTLE

NEWEL-POST LAMP IN
HAND-WROUGHT STEEL
DESIGNED AND EXECUTED
BY N. & E. SPITTLE

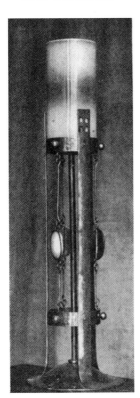

TABLE LAMP
DESIGNED BY ROBT. MACLAURIN
EXECUTED BY THE SCOTTISH
GUILD OF HANDICRAFT, LTD.

NEWEL-POST LAMP IN WROUGHT
IRON AND COPPER
DESIGNED AND EXECUTED
BY GEO. WRAGGE, LTD.

TABLE LAMP IN WROUGHT BRASS
DESIGNED BY A. STUBBS
EXECUTED BY JESSON, BIRKETT & CO., LTD.

TABLE LAMP IN WROUGHT COPPER
DESIGNED BY A. STUBBS
EXECUTED BY JESSON, BIRKETT & CO., LTD.

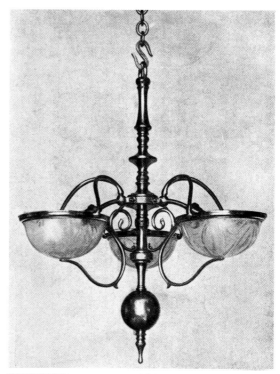

ELECTROLIER      DESIGNED AND EXECUTED BY
W. A. S. BENSON & CO., LTD.

ELECTROLIER IN HAMMERED BRASS
DESIGNED AND EXECUTED BY PERRY & CO.

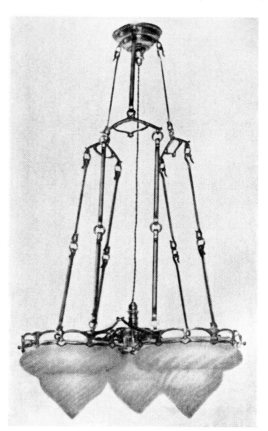

ELECTROLIER      DESIGNED AND EXECUTED
BY W. A. S. BENSON & CO., LTD.

ELECTROLIER IN     DESIGNED BY W. PIDDINGTON
OXYDISED SILVER    EXECUTED BY THOS. BRAWN & CO.

ELECTROLIER      DESIGNED BY P. A. HILL
IN BRONZE        EXECUTED BY N. & E. SPITTLE

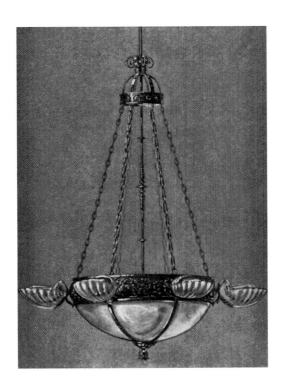

ELECTROLIER IN    DESIGNED AND EXECUTED
STEEL BRONZE     BY PERRY & CO.

GAS PENDANT IN WROUGHT BRONZE.   DESIGNED
BY C. A. LL. ROBERTS, EXECUTED BY E. & R. GITTINS

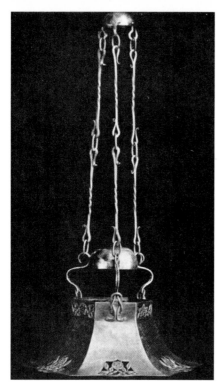

HANGING LAMP DESIGNED BY R. HIL-
TON, EXECUTED BY THE KESWICK
SCHOOL OF INDUSTRIAL ARTS

ELECTROLIER IN BRONZE DE-
SIGNED BY PERCY A. HILL, EXE-
CUTED BY N. AND E. SPITAL

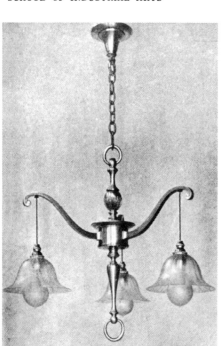

ELECTROLIER IN BRONZE DESIGNED
BY PERCY A. HILL, EXECUTED BY
N. AND E. SPITAL

HANGING LAMP IN BRONZE DESIGNED
BY PERCY A. HILL, EXECUTED BY
N. AND E. SPITAL

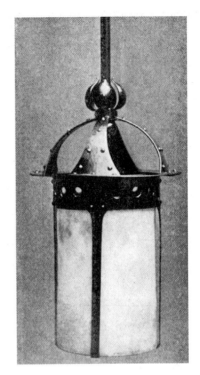

HANGING LANTERN DESIGNED BY
A. G. STUBBS, EXECUTED BY
JESSON, BIRKETT AND CO., LTD.

ELECTROLIER IN HAMMERED BRASS WITH
A SILK SHADE, DESIGNED AND EXECUTED
BY LIBERTY AND CO., LTD.

ELECTRIC LIGHT BRACKET, DESIGNED
AND EXECUTED BY THE WELL FIRE
CO., LTD.

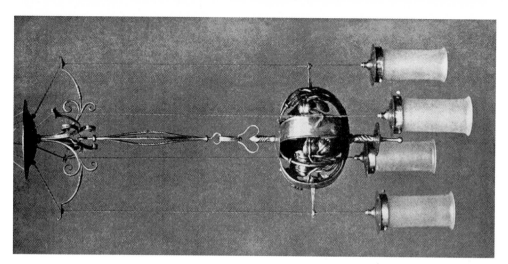

ELECTRIC PENDANT IN WROUGHT
IRON DESIGNED AND EXECUTED
BY W. BAINBRIDGE REYNOLDS, LTD.

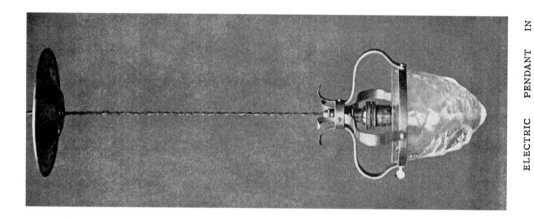

ELECTRIC PENDANT IN
BRONZE DESIGNED BY C. F. A.
VOYSEY, EXECUTED BY W.
BAINBRIDGE REYNOLDS, LTD.

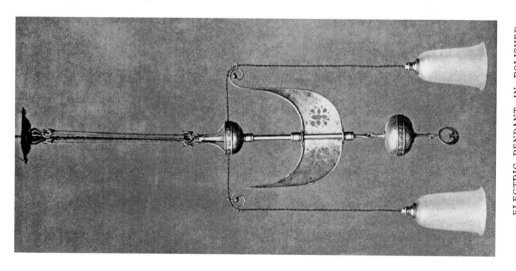

ELECTRIC PENDANT IN POLISHED
IRON DESIGNED AND EXECUTED
BY W. BAINBRIDGE REYNOLDS, LTD.

GAS, OIL AND ELECTRIC PENDANTS
DESIGNED BY A. G. STUBBS, EXECUTED
BY JESSON, BIRKETT AND CO., LTD.

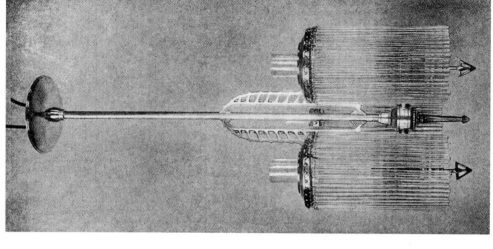

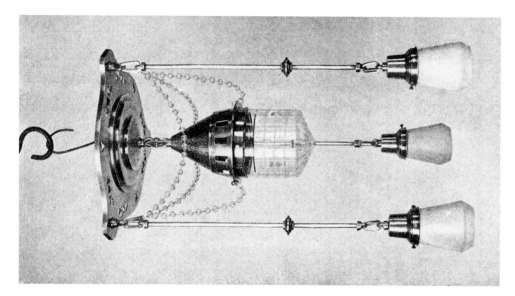

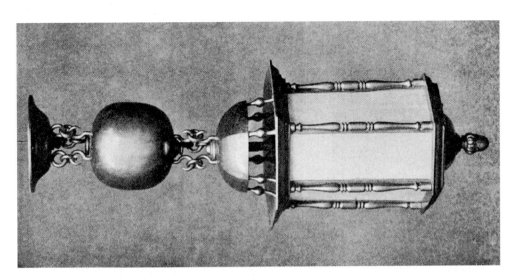

HANGING LAMP IN BRASS DESIGNED AND EXECUTED BY W. BAINBRIDGE REYNOLDS, LTD.

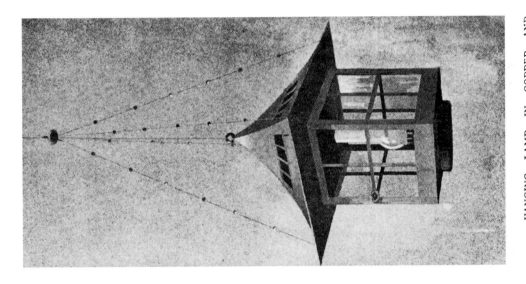

HANGING LAMP IN COPPER AND WROUGHT IRON DESIGNED BY PERCY LANCASTER, EXECUTED BY W. LAN-CASTER

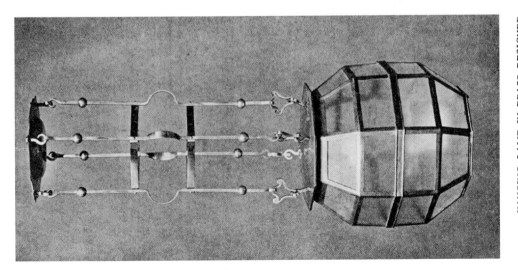

HANGING LAMP IN BRASS DESIGNED AND EXECUTED BY W. BAINBRIDGE REYNOLDS, LTD.

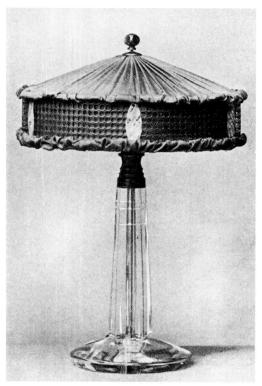

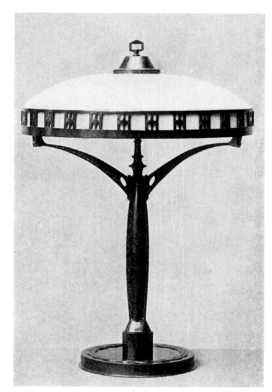

DESIGNED BY PAUL BISCHOFF

DESIGNED BY BERNHARD WENIG

DESIGNED BY PAUL BISCHOFF

DESIGNED BY PAUL BISCHOFF

BRONZE ELECTRIC TABLE LAMPS EXECUTED BY RICHARD L. F. SCHULZ

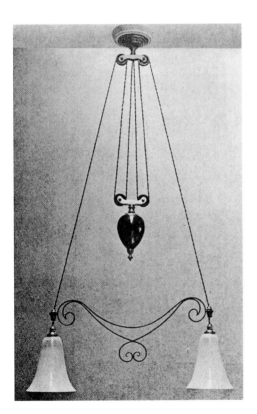

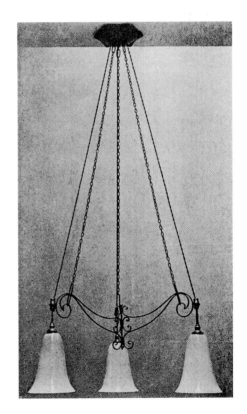

ELECTRIC LIGHT FITTINGS DESIGNED
AND EXECUTED BY JAMES POWELL AND
SONS (WHITEFRIARS GLASS WORKS)

ELECTRIC SCONCE IN BRONZE-GILT. DESIGNED BY
EDWARD SPENCER, EXECUTED BY CHAS. MOXEY, OF THE ARTIFICERS' GUILD

CANDLE PENDANT IN PAINTED AND LACQUERED WOOD, FOR A NURSERY
DESIGNED BY EDWARD SPENCER, PAINTED BY G. SPINK, OF THE ARTIFICERS' GUILD

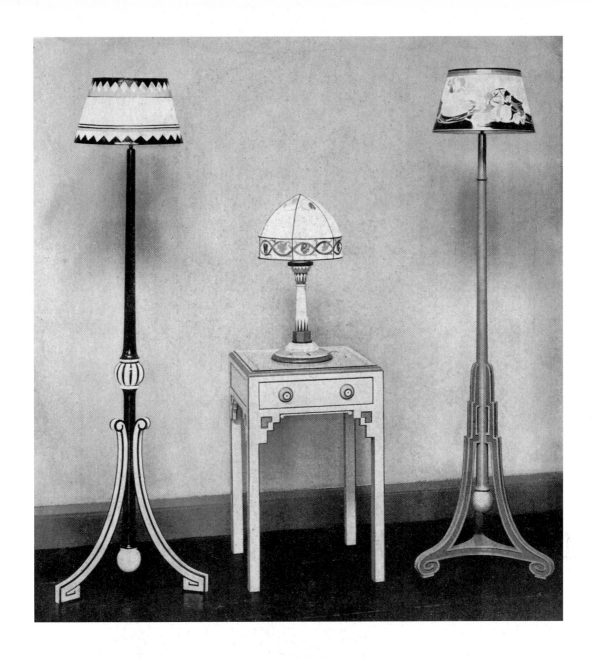

PAINTED FURNITURE. DESIGNED BY
THE LATE LIEUT. NOEL SIMMONS

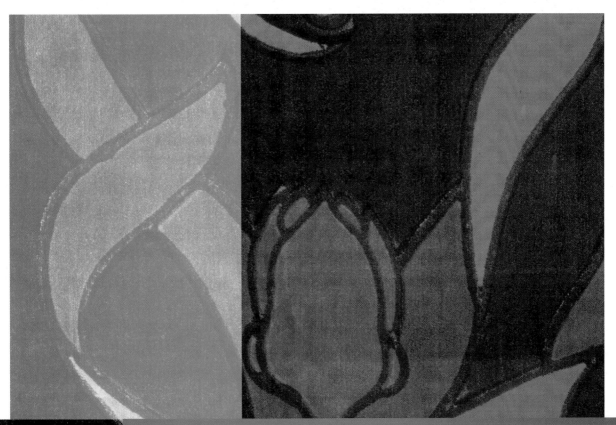

textiles and wall decoration | Stoffe und Wanddekoration | Textiles et décorations murales

SILK AND COTTON  DESIGNED AND EXECUTED
TAPESTRY     BY LIBERTY & CO., LTD.

THE "VINE" WOOL TAPESTRY
     DESIGNED BY J. H. DEARLE
     EXECUTED BY MORRIS & CO., LTD.

WOOL TAPESTRY  DESIGNED BY CECIL MILLAR
       EXECUTED BY STORY & CO.

SILK BROCADE  DESIGNED BY CECIL MILLAR
       EXECUTED BY J. J. PAYNE & CO.

SILK TAPESTRY              DESIGNED AND EXECUTED
BY LIBERTY & CO., LTD.

SILK TAPESTRY              DESIGNED AND EXECUTED
BY LIBERTY & CO., LTD.

WOOL TAPESTRY          DESIGNED AND EXECUTED
BY LIBERTY & CO., LTD.

SILK AND COTTON        DESIGNED AND EXECUTED
TAPESTRY                   BY LIBERTY & CO., LTD.

EMBROIDERED PANEL AND CUSHION DESIGNED BY ANN MACBETH.
SEWN BY GERTRUDE YOUNG AND KATE CATTERALL.

THE "GREVILLE"    DESIGNED AND EXECUTED
WALL-PAPER    BY ESSEX & CO., LTD.

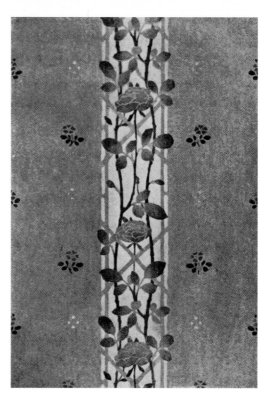

THE "ROSE STRIPE"    DESIGNED BY J. ILLINGWORTH KAY
WALL-PAPER    EXECUTED BY ESSEX & CO., LTD.

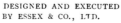

THE "SYON"    DESIGNED BY T. R. SPENCE
WALL-PAPER    EXECUTED BY ESSEX & CO., LTD.

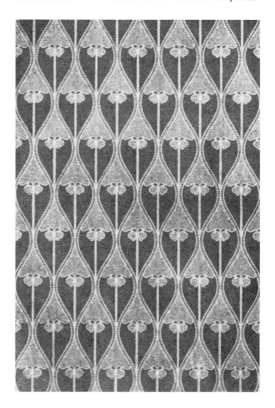

THE "PINNER"    DESIGNED AND EXECUTED
WALL-PAPER    BY ESSEX & CO., LTD.

THE "OLD WOMAN WHO LIVED
IN A SHOE" WALL-PAPER
   DESIGNED BY WILL KIDD
   EXECUTED BY ARTHUR SANDERSON & SONS

THE "SIR WALTER" WALL-PAPER
   DESIGNED BY L. STAHL
   EXECUTED BY ARTHUR SANDERSON & SONS

THE "LOLLARD" WALL-PAPER
   DESIGNED BY L. STAHL
   EXECUTED BY ARTHUR SANDERSON & SONS

THE "PIGEONS" WALL-PAPER
   DESIGNED BY WILL KIDD
   EXECUTED BY ARTHUR SANDERSON & SONS

THE "BURCOT" DESIGNED BY C. K. LENNOX
WALL-PAPER     EXECUTED BY C. KNOWLES & CO., LTD.

THE "KYNASTON" DESIGNED BY WILLIAM TURNER
WALL-PAPER     EXECUTED BY C. KNOWLES & CO., LTD.

THE "EVERLEY" DESIGNED BY THOMAS TURNER
WALL-PAPER     EXECUTED BY C. KNOWLES & CO , LTD.

THE "CELTIC DESIGNED BY ARTHUR WILCOCK
ROSE" WALL-PAPER   EXECUTED BY C. KNOWLES & CO., LTD.

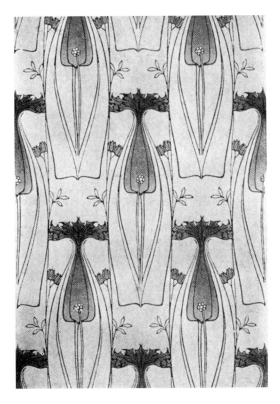

THE "PORTLEDGE"
WALL-PAPERS

DESIGNED BY HARRY NAPPER
EXECUTED BY ROTTMANN & CO.

THE "ROBIN HOOD"
WALL-PAPER

DESIGNED BY HARRY NAPPER
EXECUTED BY ROTTMANN & CO.

THE "IRIS POND"
WALL-PAPER

DESIGNED BY G. R. RIGBY
EXECUTED BY ROTTMANN & CO.

THE "WHITWOOD"
WALL-PAPER

DESIGNED BY HARRY NAPPER
EXECUTED BY ROTTMANN & CO.

THE " LOUISE " FRIEZE

DESIGNED BY HARRY NAPPER
EXECUTED BY ROTTMANN & CO.

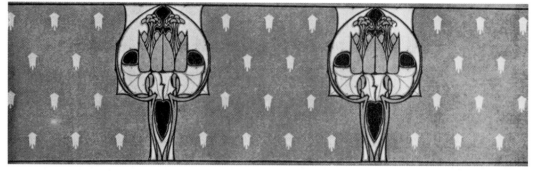

THE " ROSSETTI " FRIEZE

DESIGNED BY MANSELL H. JONES
EXECUTED BY ROTTMANN & CO.

THE " YETMINSTER "
WALL-PAPER

DESIGNED BY HARRY NAPPER
EXECUTED BY ROTTMANN & CO.

THE " CHURSTON "
WALL-PAPER

DESIGNED BY HARRY NAPPER
EXECUTED BY ROTTMANN & CO.

THE "POMEGRANATE" FRIEZE

DESIGNED BY MANSELL H. JONES
EXECUTED BY ROTTMANN & CO.

THE "IRENE" FRIEZE

DESIGNED BY HARRY NAPPER
EXECUTED BY ROTTMANN & CO.

THE "ST. AUSTELL"
WALL-PAPER

DESIGNED BY HARRY NAPPER
EXECUTED BY ROTTMANN & CO.

THE "FIG TREE"
WALL-PAPER

DESIGNED BY M. B. JONES
EXECUTED BY ROTTMANN & CO.

PORTION OF AN EMBROIDERED CASEMENT CURTAIN. DESIGNED
BY ANN MACBETH, WORKED BY GERTRUDE ANDERSON

EMBROIDERED AND APPLIQUÉ PANEL            DESIGNED AND WORKED BY HELENA SHAW

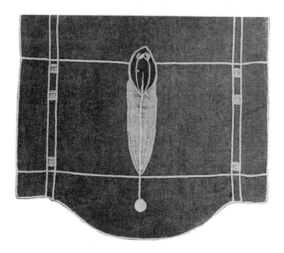

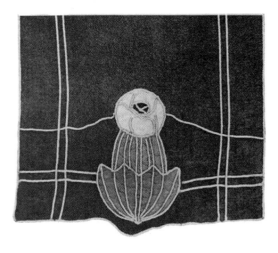

ENDS OF APPLIQUÉ TABLE CENTRES            DESIGNED BY H. DAVIS RICHTER

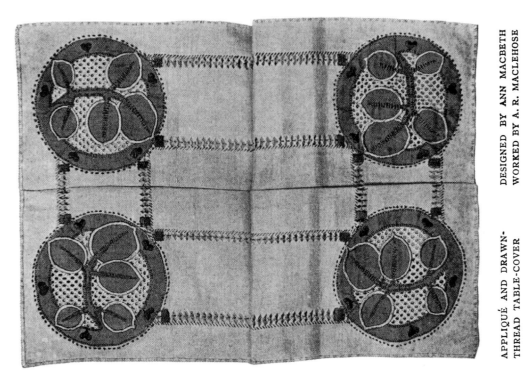

DESIGNED BY ANN MACBETH
WORKED BY A. R. MACLEHOSE

APPLIQUÉ AND DRAWN-
THREAD TABLE-COVER

DESIGNED AND WORKED
BY GWENDOLIN PARRY

EMBROIDERED AND APPLIQUÉ
CUSHION COVER

THE "BIANCA" WALL-PAPER. DESIGNED BY
I. KAY, EXECUTED BY ESSEX AND CO., LTD.

THE "WALDEN" WALL-PAPER. DESIGNED BY
I. KAY, EXECUTED BY ESSEX AND CO., LTD.

THE "BRUCE" WALL-PAPER. DESIGNED BY E. L.
PATTISON, EXECUTED BY ESSEX AND CO., LTD.

THE "ABINGWORTH" WALL-PAPER. DESIGNED
BY I. KAY, EXECUTED BY ESSEX AND CO., LTD.

WALL-PAPER DESIGNED BY G. R. RIGBY, EXE-
CUTED BY JEFFREY AND CO.

THE "LOCKSLEY" WALL-PAPER. DESIGNED BY
SIDNEY MAWSON, EXECUTED BY JEFFREY AND CO.

WALL-PAPER DESIGNED BY HEYWOOD SUMNER,
EXECUTED BY JEFFREY AND CO.

WALL-PAPER DESIGNED BY E. McCLELLAND,
EXECUTED BY C. KNOWLES AND CO., LTD.

THE "WOLSELEY" WALL-PAPER. DESIGNED BY W. HUTT, EXECUTED BY C. KNOWLES AND CO., LTD.

THE "ALDERLEY" WALL-PAPER. DESIGNED BY R. SILVER, EXECUTED BY C. KNOWLES AND CO., LTD.

THE "CHETWYND" WALL-PAPER. DESIGNED BY J. WOOD, EXECUTED BY JOHN LINE AND SONS, LTD.

WALL-PAPER DESIGNED BY SYDNEY HAWARD EXECUTED BY JOHN LINE AND SONS, LTD.

WALL-PAPER DESIGNED AND EXECUTED
BY ARTHUR SANDERSON AND SONS, LTD.

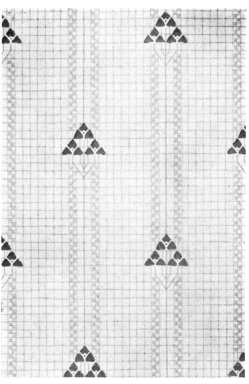

WALL-PAPER DESIGNED AND EXECUTED
BY ARTHUR SANDERSON AND SONS, LTD.

WALL-PAPER DESIGNED AND EXECUTED
BY ARTHUR SANDERSON AND SONS, LTD.

WALL-PAPER DESIGNED AND EXECUTED
BY ARTHUR SANDERSON AND SONS, LTD.

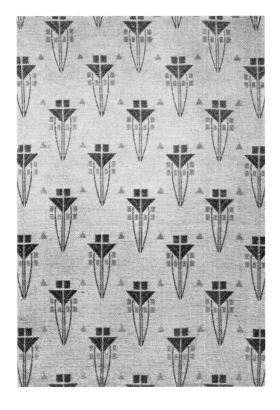

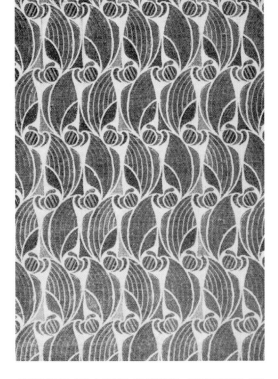

FURNITURE TAPESTRIES

DESIGNED BY LOTTE FOCHLER, EXECUTED BY
P. HAAS UND SÖHNE

CUSHIONS DESIGNED BY L. FÖRSTNER, EXECUTED
BY THE PRAG RUDNIKER WERKSTÄTTE, VIENNA

WALL-PAPER DESIGNED BY C. F. A. VOY-
SEY, EXECUTED BY A. SANDERSON AND SONS, LTD.

WALL-PAPER DESIGNED BY SIDNEY
HAWARD, EXECUTED BY JEFFREY AND CO.

WALL-PAPER DESIGNED BY SIDNEY
HAWARD, EXECUTED BY JEFFREY AND CO.

WALL-PAPER DESIGNED BY C. F. A. VOY-
SEY, EXECUTED BY A. SANDERSON AND SONS, LTD.

BROCADE

DESIGNED BY ARCH. OTTO PRUTSCHER,
EXECUTED BY J. BACKHAUSEN UND SÖHNE

END PAPER FOR
BLOTTER

DESIGNED AND EXECUTED BY
ARCH. OTTO PRUTSCHER

DESIGN FOR A CAR-
PET BY VALENTIN
HRDLICKA, ARCHI-
TECT

WOOL TAPESTRY DESIGNED BY
PROF. HOFFMANN, EXECUTED BY
J. BACKHAUSEN UND SÖHNE

COTTON TAPESTRY DESIGNED
BY PROF. HOFFMANN, EXECUTED
BY J. BACKHAUSEN UND SÖHNE

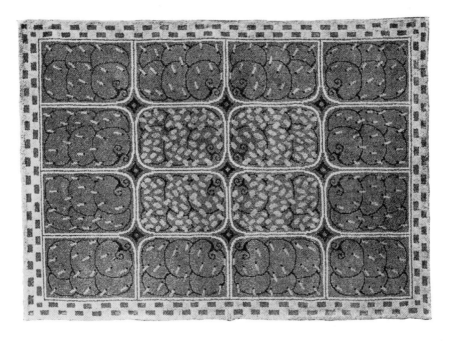

CARPET DESIGNED BY GERTRUD KLEINHEMPEL EXE-
CUTED BY THE WERKSTÄTTEN FÜR DEUTSCHEN HAUS-
RAT (THEOPHIL MÜLLER,) DRESDEN-STRIESEN

HAND-TUFTED SMYRNA CARPET DESIGNED BY
PROF. ERICH KLEINHEMPEL, EXECUTED BY THE
WURZNER CARPET MANUFACTURING CO.

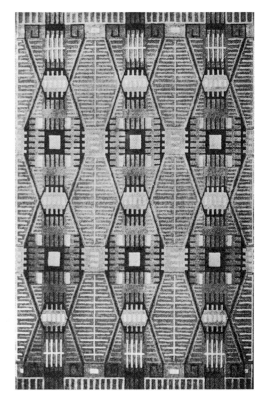

HAND-TUFTED SMYRNA CARPET DESIGNED BY
GERTRUD KLEINHEMPEL EXECUTED BY THE
WURZNER CARPET MANUFACTURING CO.

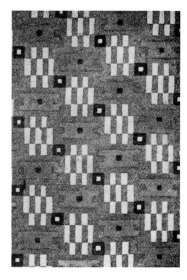

WOVEN FABRICS                                DESIGNED BY EMIL PIRCHAN, ARCHITECT

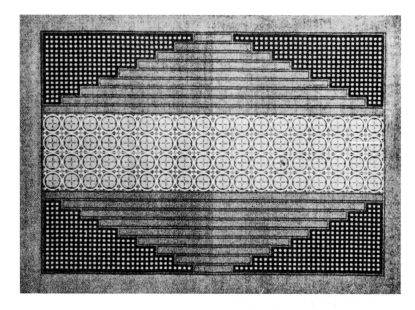

CARPET DESIGNED BY PROF. OTTO PRUTSCHER
EXECUTED BY HERRBERGER UND RHOMBERG

WOOL TAPESTRY DESIGNED BY PAUL ROLLER, ARCHI-
TECT, EXECUTED BY J. BACKHAUSEN UND SÖHNE

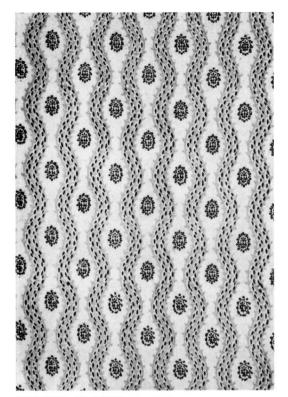

DESIGNED BY LOTTE FOCHLER

DESIGNED BY CARL WITZMANN

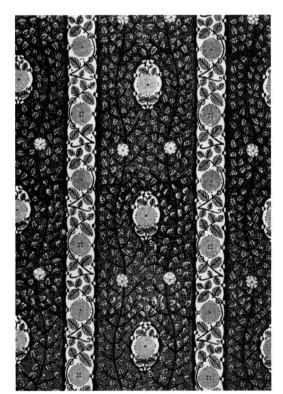

DESIGNED BY ADOLF HOLUB

DESIGNED BY E. MARGOLD

CRETONNES EXECUTED BY JOH. BACKHAUSEN UND SÖHNE

DESIGNED BY PROF. JOSEF HOFFMANN

DESIGNED BY PROF. OTTO PRUTSCHER

DESIGNED BY H. GEIRINGER

DESIGNED BY PAUL ROLLER

TAPESTRIES EXECUTED BY JOH. BACKHAUSEN UND SÖHNE

CARPET DESIGNED BY FRANZ MESSNER AND BRO-
CADES DESIGNED BY PROF. JOSEF HOFFMANN EX-
ECUTED BY JOH. BACKHAUSEN UND SÖHNE

EMBROIDERED COVERLET
DESIGNED BY ANN MAC-
BETH, SEWN BY MARY
MACBETH

ALTAR FRONTAL FOR S. MARY'S CATHE-
DRAL, GLASGOW, SHOWING DETAIL
OF CENTRE, DESIGNED BY ANN MAC-
BETH, SEWN BY AGNES E. P. SKENE.

ARRAS TAPESTRY WALL PANEL DESIGNED BY H. DEARLE
EXECUTED BY MORRIS AND CO., LTD.

ARRAS TAPESTRY—"LOVE AND THE PILGRIM"    DESIGNED BY SIR E. BURNE-JONES, BART.
EXECUTED BY MORRIS AND CO., LTD.

ARRAS TAPESTRY PORTIÈRE DESIGNED BY
H. DEARLE, EXECUTED BY MORRIS AND CO., LTD.

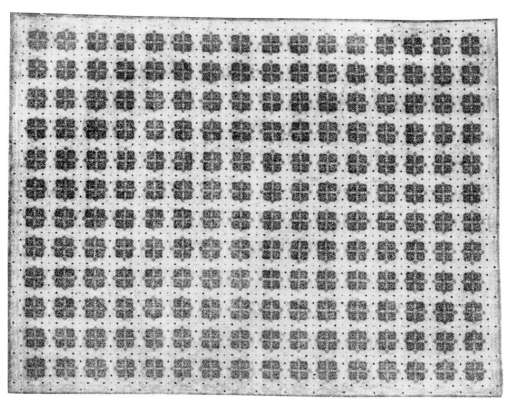

HAND-MADE SMYRNA CARPET          DESIGNED BY PROF. BRUNO PAUL

CARPET DESIGNED BY PROF. BRUNO PAUL

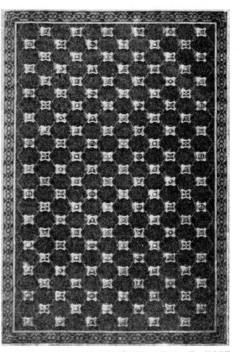

CARPET DESIGNED BY A. E. KOFF

CARPETS EXECUTED BY THE VEREINIGTE
SMYRNA-TEPPICH-FABRIKEN, BERLIN

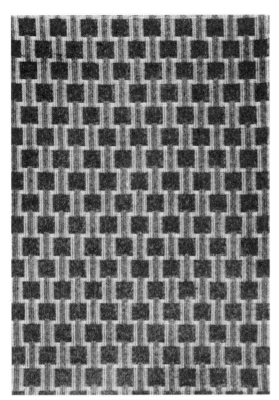

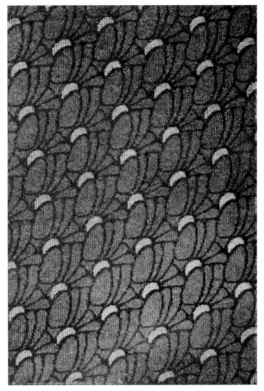

DESIGNED BY DEBSCHITZ AND LOCHNER

DESIGNED BY RAIMUND JAHN

DESIGNED BY GUSTAV KOTTMANN

DESIGNED BY HERMANN EHLERS

WOVEN FABRICS EXECUTED BY GUSTAV KOTTMANN

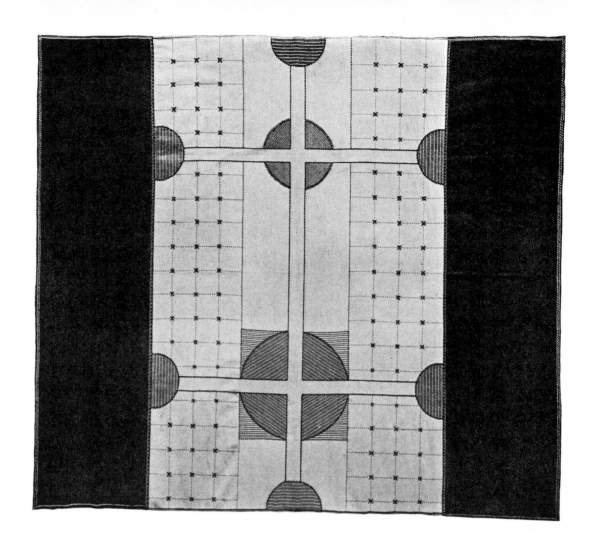

EMBROIDERED    BEDSPREAD
DESIGNED  BY  ANN  MACBETH
SEWN  BY  A.  HENDRY

FRONTAL FOR S. BARTHOLOMEW'S CHURCH. HASLEMERE.
DESIGNED BY ANN MACBETH, EXECUTED BY SOME HASLEMERE LADIES.

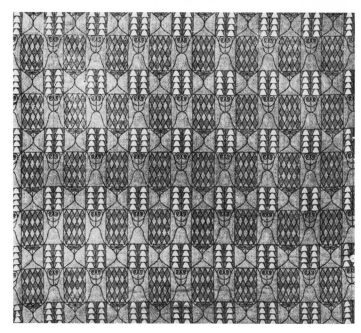

DESIGNED BY PROF. JOSEF HOFFMANN

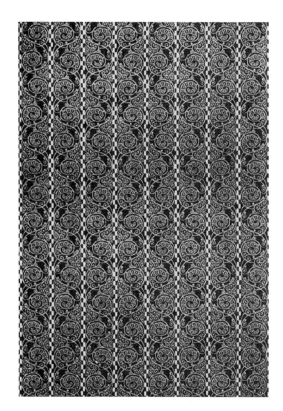

DESIGNED BY PAUL ROLLER

DESIGNED BY PROF. JOSEF HOFFMANN

BROCADES EXECUTED BY JOH.
BACKHAUSEN UND SÖHNE

CARPET DESIGNED BY PROF. CHRISTIANSEN
EXECUTED BY J. GINZKEY

CARPET DESIGNED BY PROF. ERICH KLEINHAMPEL
EXECUTED BY J. GINZKEY

CORNER OF A CARPET DESIGNED BY PROF.
OTTO PRUTSCHER, EXECUTED BY J. GINZKEY

CORNER OF A BED-SPREAD DESIGNED BY LOTTE
FOCHLER, EXECUTED BY GEBRÜDER ROSENTHAL

EMBROIDERED CUSHION DESIGNED
AND SEWN BY M. L. FANGRIEVE

EMBROIDERED CUSHION DESIGNED
AND SEWN BY AMELIA R. HUTCHISON

DESIGNED BY PROF. ALBIN MÜLLER

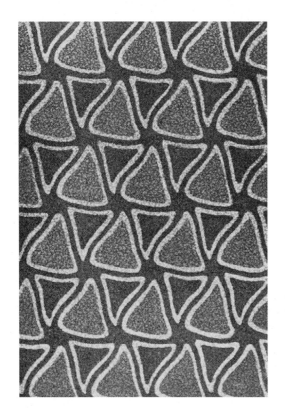

DESIGNED BY PROF. ALBIN MÜLLER

DESIGNED BY KARL EEG, B.D.A.

LINOLEUM EXECUTED BY THE DEL-
MENHORSTER LINOLEUM-FABRIK

WOVEN TABLE-COVERS DESIGNED BY PROF. OTTO PRUTSCHER, EXECUTED BY HERRBURGER UND RHOMBERG

CORNERS OF TABLE-COVERS DESIGNED BY PROF. A. BOHLA, EXECUTED BY NORBERT LANGER UND SÖHNE

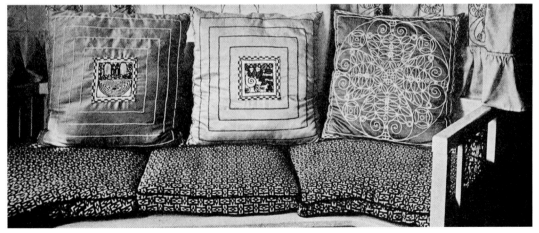

EMBROIDERED CUSHIONS DESIGNED BY GOTTFRIED CZERMAK, SEWN BY LILLY SPITZ

CHAIR SEAT IN TENT-STITCH
DESIGNED BY FREDERICK VIGERS
EXECUTED BY C. PALMER-KERRISON

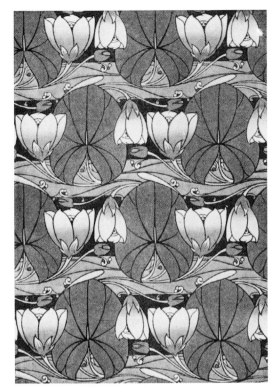

CRETONNES DESIGNED BY HARRY NAPPER, EXECUTED BY G. P. AND J. BAKER, LTD.

WOVEN TAPESTRIES DESIGNED BY FREDERICK VIGERS, EXECUTED BY ALEX. MORTON AND CO.

CRETONNE DESIGNED BY W. MARTENS

CRETONNE DESIGNED BY W. MARTENS

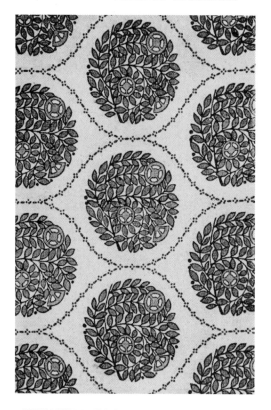

CRETONNE DESIGNED BY HELENE GEIRINGER

TAPESTRY DESIGNED BY W. MARTENS

TEXTILE FABRICS EXECUTED BY JOH. BACKHAUSEN UND SÖHNE

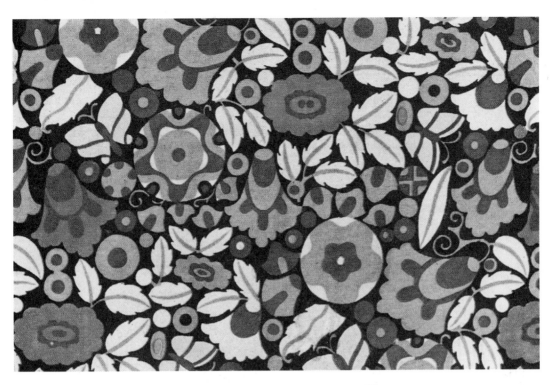

DESIGNED BY ED. WIMMER, ARCHITECT.

DESIGNED BY LOTTE FROEMMEL-FOCHLER.

PRINTED SILKS EXECUTED BY THE WIENER WERKSTAETTE.

DESIGN FOR AN EMBROIDERED PANEL FOR OVERMANTEL BY MURIEL BOYD

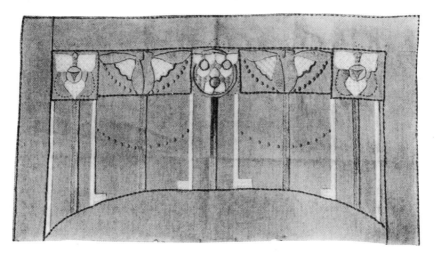

EMBROIDERED CHAIR-BACK COVER DESIGNED AND SEWN BY
ANNIE S. PATERSON

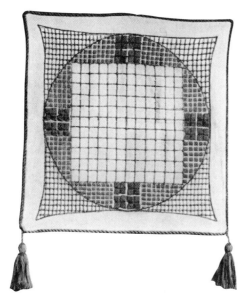

CUSHION AND BLOTTER DESIGNED AND SEWN BY ANNIE S. PATERSON

· LEST · THE · SOVL · OF · YVONNE · SHOVLD · STRAY · AND · BE · LOST · FOREVER · THERE · IN · THE · DEEP · IN · THE · WONDERFVL · HILLS · OF · SLEEP ·

DESIGN FOR A PANEL IN GESSO, FOR A BEDROOM DECORATION. BY JESSIE M. KING

"ST. ELIZABETH"—EMBROIDERED PANEL DESIGNED
BY ANN MACBETH, SEWN BY ELIZABETH WOOD.

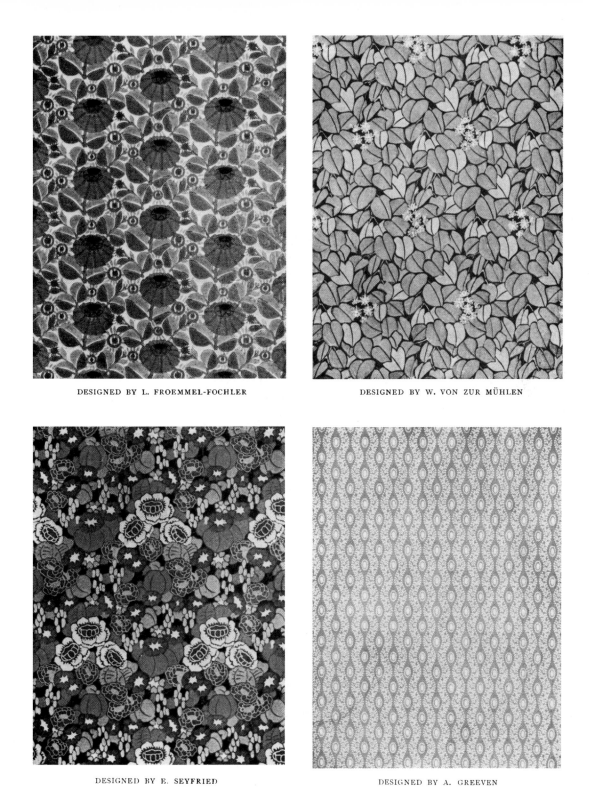

DESIGNED BY L. FROEMMEL-FOCHLER

DESIGNED BY W. VON ZUR MÜHLEN

DESIGNED BY E. SEYFRIED

DESIGNED BY A. GREEVEN

WALLPAPERS EXECUTED BY ERISMANN AND COMPANY

DESIGNED BY PROF. JOSEF HOFFMANN

DESIGNED BY PROF. JOSEF HOFFMANN

DESIGNED BY JOSEF ZOTTI

DESIGNED BY JOSEF ZOTTI

HAND-PRINTED LINENS EXECUTED BY S. E. STEINER AND CO.

DESIGNED BY PROF. LUDWIG JUNGNICKEL

DESIGNED BY LOTTE FOCHLER

DESIGNED BY LOTTE FOCHLER

DESIGNED BY LOTTE FOCHLER

PRINTED SILKS EXECUTED BY THE WIENER WERKSTAETTE

DESIGNED BY PROF. JOSEF HOFFMANN

DESIGNED BY PROF. C. O. CZESCHKA

PRINTED SILKS EXECUTED BY
THE WIENER WERKSTAETTE

PRINTED SILKS DESIGNED BY PH. HÄUSLER
EXECUTED BY WILHELM METZER

SILK WITH BATIK DECORATION. DE-
SIGNED BY PROF. ARTUR LAKATÓS,
EXECUTED BY KLARA ROMAN

PRINTED VELVET DESIGNED BY P. BAUDRIER
EXECUTED BY JACQUES RUHLMANN

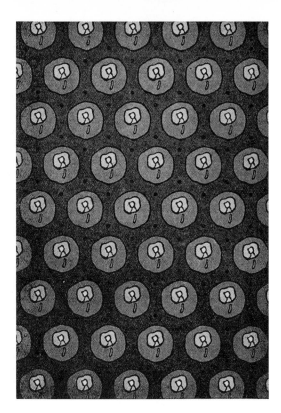

WALLPAPER DESIGNED AND EXECUTED
BY "MARTINE"

WALLPAPER DESIGNED AND EXECUTED
BY JACQUES RUHLMANN

EMBROIDERED TABLE-CENTRE

DESIGNED AND EXECUTED BY JOHN JACOBSON

DESIGNED BY GEORGE BARBIER

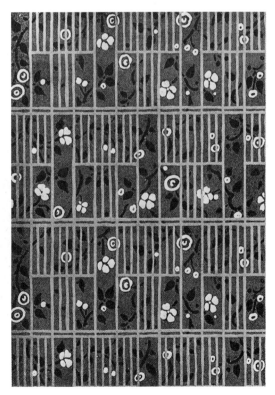

DESIGNED BY ANDRÉ GROULT

DESIGNED BY GEORGE BARBIER

DESIGNED BY GEORGES D'ESPAGNAT

WALLPAPERS EXECUTED BY ANDRÉ GROULT

DESIGN FOR AN EMBROIDERED PANEL FOR THE OVERMANTEL OF A MORNING-ROOM. BY JESSIE M. KING

HE·WANDERS·IN·A·HAPPY·DREAM·THROUGH·SCENTED·GOLDEN·HOURS·

HE·FLUTES·TO·WOO·A·FAIRY·LOVE·KNEE·DEEP·IN·FAIRY·FLOWERS

TIR·NAN·OG

"FOR LO! THE WINTER IS PAST, THE RAIN IS OVER AND GONE"
LUNETTE DECORATION IN TEMPERA. BY JESSIE BAYES, R.M.S.

THE "COLUMBINE," DESIGNED BY ALLAN F. VIGERS

THE "ROSA RUGUSA," DESIGNED BY HEYWOOD SUMNER

THE "MACAW," DESIGNED BY WALTER CRANE

THE "MIKADO," DESIGNED BY ALBERT GRIFFITHS

WALLPAPERS EXECUTED BY JEFFREY AND CO.

THE " HADDON " AND " PEONY," WALLPAPERS DESIGNED FOR LIBERTY AND CO.

THE " BLENHEIM," DESIGNED BY FREDERICK VIGERS     THE " IRIS," DESIGNED BY J. R. HOUGHTON
WALLPAPERS EXECUTED BY JEFFREY AND CO.

THE "FAIRYLAND," DESIGNED BY C. F. A. VOYSEY
WALLPAPER EXECUTED BY ESSEX AND CO.

WALLPAPER DESIGNED BY H. WATKINS WILD
EXECUTED BY A. SANDERSON AND SONS

THE "ELIZABETH'S GARDEN," DESIGNED BY S. HAWARD

THE "WELBECK," DESIGNED BY EDGAR L. PATTISON

WALLPAPERS EXECUTED BY JOHN LINE AND SONS

THE "MENTONE" AND "MONTAGUE," WALLPAPERS DESIGNED AND EXECUTED BY SHAND KYDD

THE "LEICESTER," DESIGNED BY H. DEARLE
WALLPAPER EXECUTED BY MORRIS AND CO.

THE "RANMORE," WALLPAPER DESIGNED AND
EXECUTED BY SHAND KYDD

PAINTED NURSERY-PANELS
BY CARLE MICHEL BOOG

Jack Sprat, Had a cat, It had but one ear,
It went to buy butter, When butter was dear.

The Frog Prince.

King Thrushbeard.

PAINTED NURSERY-PANELS
BY CARLE MICHEL BOOG

WHATSOEVER·TH
HAND·FINDETH
TO·DO:DO·WITH
ALL·THY·MICHT

EMBROIDERED PORTIÈRE. DESIGNED
AND SEWN BY WILHELMINA EDELSTEIN
(HAMMERSMITH SCHOOL OF ARTS & CRAFTS)

*(Under the direction of Mr. and
Mrs. Reginald Frampton)*

PORTION OF EMBROIDERED HANGING. DESIGNED BY G. LL. MORRIS
SEWN BY WINIFRED MORRIS. COLOUR SCHEME BY FANNY BECKETT

THE "INTERTWINE" TAPESTRY.   DESIGNED BY EDMUND HUNTER, EXECUTED BY THE ST. EDMUNDSBURY WEAVERS

THE "ORCHARD" DAMASK.   DESIGNED BY EDMUND HUNTER, EXECUTED BY THE ST. EDMUNDSBURY WEAVERS

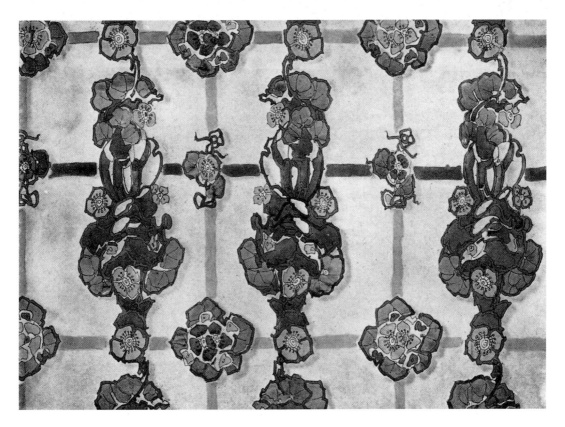

DESIGNS FOR PRINTED CRETONNES.  BY JESSIE M. KING

I chatter chatter as i flow to ioin the brimming river
For men may come and men may go but i go on for ever

"THE BROOK"—ARRAS TAPESTRY
DESIGNED BY J. H. DEARLE, EXECUTED
BY MORRIS AND COMPANY

WOVEN TAPESTRY DESIGNED AND EXECUTED
BY THE HERTER LOOMS, NEW YORK CITY

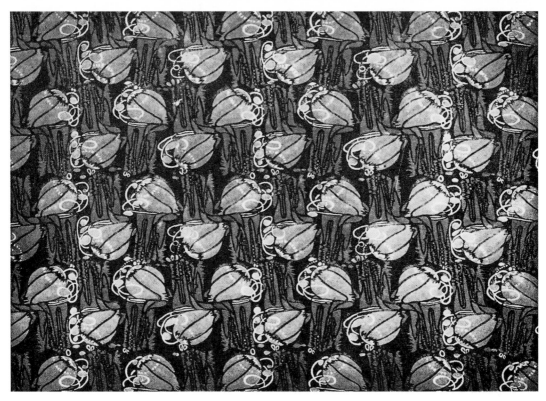

**BLOCK PRINT**                    DESIGNED BY C. MACKINTOSH, EXECUTED BY W. FOXTON

**CRETONNE**                    DESIGNED BY M. MCLEISH, EXECUTED BY W. FOXTON

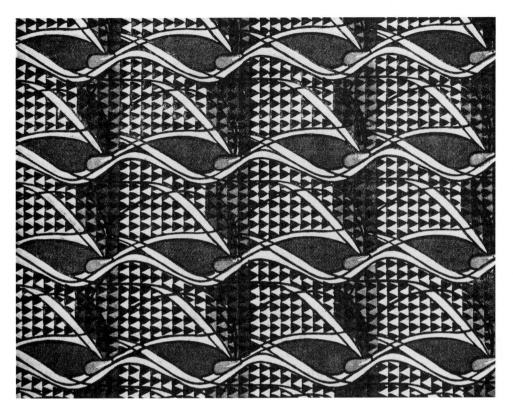

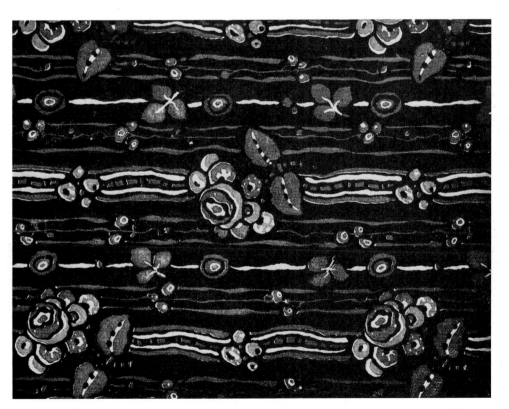

THE "BRENT" DESIGN FOR PRINTED COTTON.   BY J. H. DEARLE (MORRIS AND CO.)

THE "SHANNON" AND "RAMBLING ROSE"
DESIGNS FOR PRINTED COTTONS

BY J. H. DEARLE (MORRIS AND CO.)

THE "MILLEFLEURS" DESIGN FOR TAPESTRY
HANGING. BY J. H. DEARLE (MORRIS AND CO.)

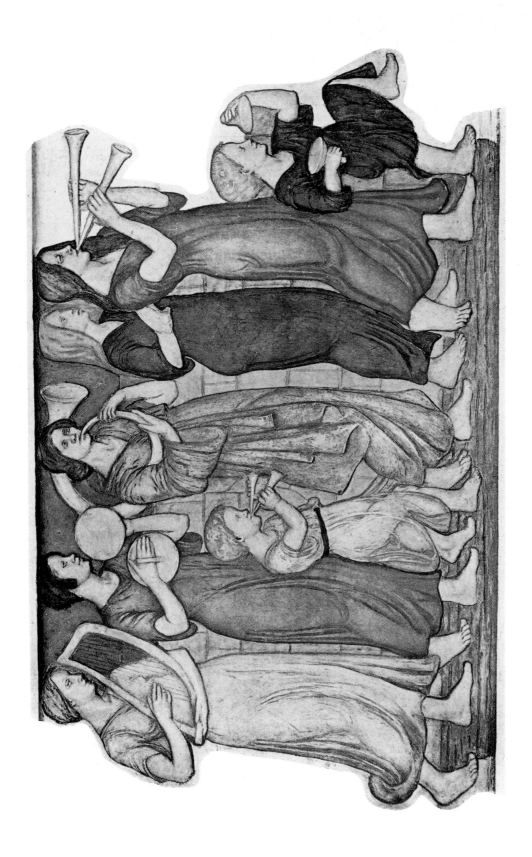

"THE WEDDING FESTIVAL"—PORTION OF COLOURED PLASTER FRIEZE. DESIGNED AND EXECUTED BY GEORGE P. BANKART

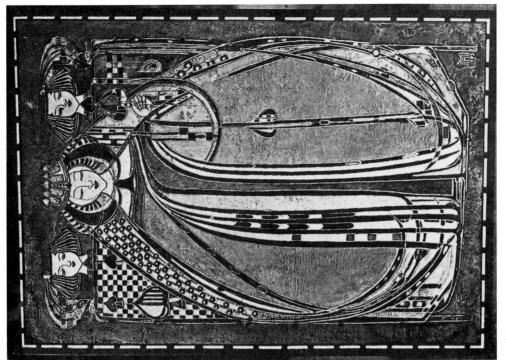

"THE QUEENS"—PANELS IN COLOURED GESSO
BY MARGARET M. MACKINTOSH, R.S.W.

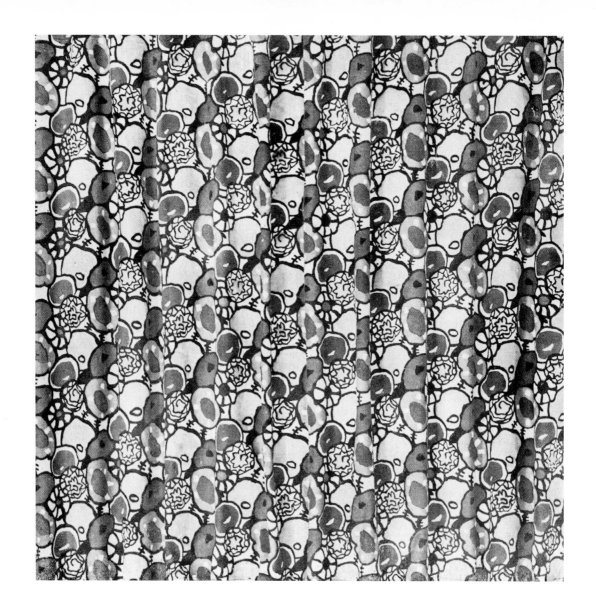

PRINTED COTTON. DESIGNED
BY MINNIE McLEISH, EXECUTED
BY W. FOXTON

CRETONNE. DESIGNED BY CONSTANCE IRVING
EXECUTED BY W. FOXTON

PRINTED COTTON. DESIGNED BY CHARLES MACKINTOSH
EXECUTED BY W. FOXTON

"THE PERSIAN DEER"—PRINTED LINEN
DESIGNED BY THE LATE C. T. LINDSAY
FOR STORY AND CO., KENSINGTON

PRINTED COTTON. DESIGNED
BY HORACE WARNER, EXECUTED
BY W. FOXTON

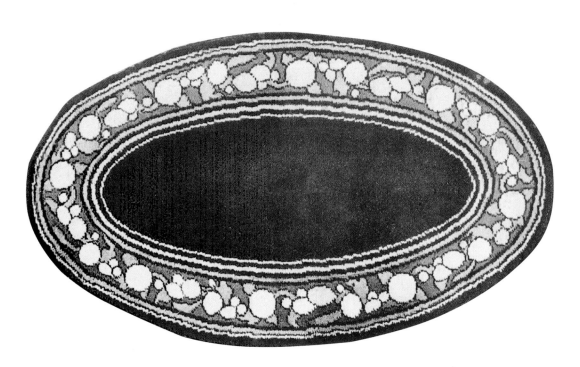

HAND-TUFTED RUGS.  DESIGNED BY
THE  LATE  LIEUT.  NOEL  SIMMONS

*From a drawing by Dora Stone*

INTERIOR SHOWING WOVEN
FABRICS BY W. FOXTON

HAND-PRINTED TISSUE. DESIGNED BY
DOROTHY HUTTON FOR W. FOXTON

MACHINE-PRINTED CRETONNE.  DESIGNED
BY J. P. BARRACLOUGH FOR W. FOXTON

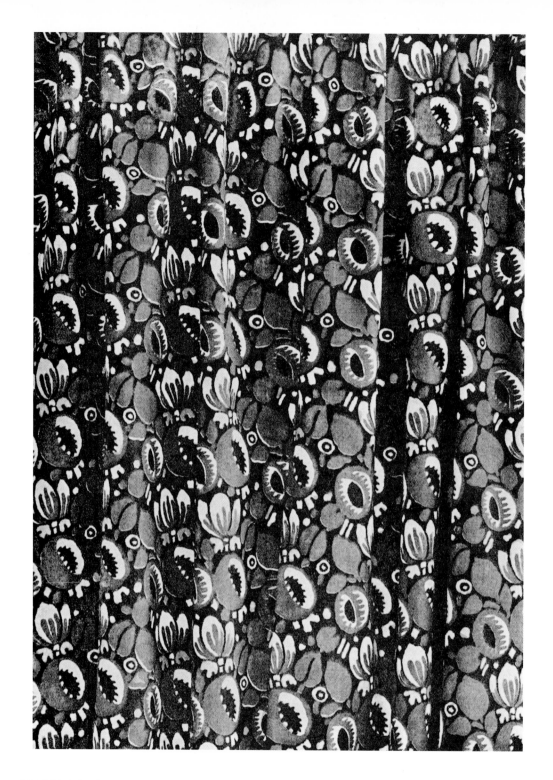

MACHINE-PRINTED CRETONNE. DESIGNED
BY M. McCLEISH FOR W. FOXTON

DESIGNED BY
CONSTANCE
IRVING

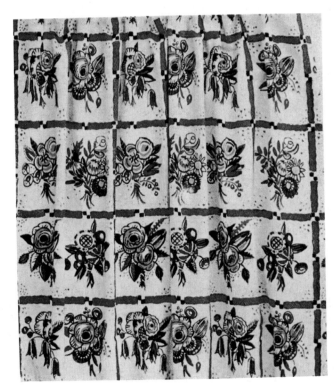

DESIGNED BY
M. McLEISH

CRETONNES BY W. FOXTON

# Index
## Designers, architects and manufacturers
## Designer, Architekten und Hersteller
## Designers, architectes et fabricants

l. = left / links / à gauche
r. = right / rechts / à droite
t. = top / oben / ci-dessus
c. = centre / Mitte
b. = / unten / ci-dessous

**Page / Seite 32:**
Charles Rennie Mackintosh, Scotland Street School, Glasgow, 1903–1906

**Page / Seite 33:**
Charles Rennie Mackintosh, Hill House, 1902–1903

**Page / Seite 270:**
Gustav Stickley, Oak double bookcase-cabinet, c. 1902

**Page / Seite 271:**
Gerrit Thomas Rietveld, *Red/Blue* chair, 1918–1923

**Page / Seite 326:**
Peter Behrens, *Aegir* wine glass, c. 1901–1905

**Page / Seite 327:**
Louis Sullivan, Leaded window for the Babson House, c. 1907

**Page / Seite 374:**
Grueby Faience Company, Earthenware vase, c. 1905

**Page / Seite 375:**
Richard Riemerschmid, Stoneware covered bowl, c. 1903

**Page / Seite 466–467:**
Tiffany Studios, *Dragonfly* hanging lamp, c. 1900–1910

**Page / Seite 438:**
George Walton, Leaded glass panel after a design of stylized roses by C. R. Mackintosh

**Page / Seite 439:**
Charles Rennie Mackintosh, Leaded mirror-glass panels, Willow Tea Rooms

**Page / Seite 482–483:**
Liberty & Co, *Tulip* textile, c. 1905

---

## Credits
## Bildnachweis
## Crédits photographiques

# DECORATIVE ART SERIES

**Decorative Art – 1900s & 1910s**
Ed. Charlotte & Peter Fiell
576 pages
3–8228–6050–6
[ENGLISH/GERMAN/FRENCH]

**Decorative Art – 1950s**
Ed. Charlotte & Peter Fiell
576 pages
3–8228–6619–9
[ENGLISH/GERMAN/FRENCH]

**Decorative Art – 1920s**
Ed. Charlotte & Peter Fiell
576 pages
3–8228–6051–4
[ENGLISH/GERMAN/FRENCH]

**Decorative Art – 1960s**
Ed. Charlotte & Peter Fiell
576 pages
3–8228–6405–6
[ENGLISH/GERMAN/FRENCH]

**Decorative Art – 1930s & 1940s**
Ed. Charlotte & Peter Fiell
576 pages
3–8228–6052–2
[ENGLISH/GERMAN/FRENCH]

**Decorative Art – 1970s**
Ed. Charlotte & Peter Fiell
576 pages
3–8228–6406–4
[ENGLISH/GERMAN/FRENCH]